TEXTS

THE ESSENTIAL
GUIDE TO
CONTEMPORARY
LITERATURE

Ian McEwan

SERIES EDITORS
Jonathan Noakes
and
Margaret Reynolds

Also available in Vintage Living Texts

Margaret Atwood
Focusing on

The Handmaid's Tale

The Blind Assassin

Bluebeard's Egg and Other Stories

Louis de Bernières
Focusing on

Captain Corelli's Mandolin

The War of Don Emmanuel's Nether Parts

Señor Vivo and the Coca Lord

The Troublesome Offspring of Cardinal Guzman

Sebastian Faulks
Focusing on

Birdsong

Charlotte Gray

The Girl at the Lion d'Or

VINTAGE
LIVING
TEXTS

Ian McEwan

THE ESSENTIAL GUIDE
TO CONTEMPORARY
LITERATURE

The Child in Time

Enduring Love

Atonement

VINTAGE

Published by Vintage 2002

6 8 10 9 7

First published in Great Britain in 2002 by Vintage
Random House, 20 Vauxhall Bridge Road,
London SW1V 2SA

www.rbooks.co.uk

Addresses for companies within
The Random House Group Limited can be found at:
www.randomhouse.co.uk/offices.htm

The Random House Group Limited Reg. No. 954009
www.randomhouse.co.uk/vintage

A CIP catalogue record for this book is available from the British Library

ISBN 9780099437550

Typeset by Palimpsest Book Production Limited, Polmont, Stirlingshire

Printed and bound in Great Britain by Clays Ltd, St Ives PL C

CONTENTS

VINTAGE LIVING TEXTS: PREFACE

IAN McEWAN

VINTAGE LIVING TEXTS

The Child in Time

Enduring Love

Atonement

VINTAGE LIVING TEXTS: REFERENCE

Acknowledgements

We owe grateful thanks to all at Random House. Most of all our debt is to Caroline Michel and her team at Vintage – especially Marcella Edwards – who have given us generous and unfailing support. Thanks also to Philippa Brewster and Georgina Capel, Michael Meredith, Angela Leighton, Harriet Marland, Louisa Joyner, Zara Warshal, to all our colleagues, and to our partners and families. We would also like to thank the teachers and students at schools and colleges around the country who have taken part in our trialling process, and who have responded so readily and warmly to our requests for advice.

And finally, our thanks to Ian McEwan for his work, without whom ... without which ...

VINTAGE
LIVING
TEXTS

Preface

About this series

Vintage Living Texts: The Essential Guide to Contemporary Literature is a new concept in reading guides. Our aim is to provide readers of all kinds with an intelligent and accessible introduction to key works of contemporary literature. Each guide suggests techniques for reading important contemporary novels, and offers a variety of back-up materials that will give you ways into the text – without ever telling you what to think.

Content

All the books reproduce an extensive interview with the author, conducted exclusively for this series. This is not to say that we believe that the author's word is law. Of course it isn't. Once his or her book has gone out into the world he or she becomes simply yet another – if singularly competent – reader. This series recognises that an author's contribution may be valuable, and intriguing, but it puts the reader in control.

Every title in the series is author-focused and covers at

least three of their novels, along with relevant biographical, bibliographical, contextual and comparative material.

How to use this series

In the reading activities that make up the core of each book you will see that you are asked to do two things. One comes from the text; that is, we suggest what you should focus on, whether it's a theme, the language or the narrative method. The other concentrates on your own response. We want you to think about how you are reading and what skills you are bringing to bear in doing that reading. So this part is very much about you, the reader.

The point is that there are many ways of responding to a text. You could concentrate on the methods you might use to compare this text with others. In that case, look for the sections headed 'Compare'. Or you might want to do something more individual, and analyse how you are reacting to a text and what it means to you, in which case, pick out the approaches labelled 'Imagine' or 'Ask Yourself'.

Of course, it may well be that you are reading these texts for an examination. In that case you will have to go for the more traditional methods of literary criticism and look for the responses that tell you to 'Discuss' or 'Analyse'. Whichever level you (or your students) are at, you will find that there is something here for everyone. However, we're not suggesting that you stick solely to the approaches we offer, or that you tackle all of the exercises laid out here. Choose whatever most interests you, or whatever best suits your purposes.

Who are these books for?

Students will find that these guides are like a good teacher. They introduce the life and work of the author, set each novel in its context, explain key ideas and literary critical terms as they arise, suggest comparative exercises in a number of media, and ask focused questions to encourage a well-informed, analytical approach to reading the novels in a way that is rigorous, but still entertaining.

Teachers will find in this series a rich source of ideas for teaching contemporary novels and their contexts, particularly at AS, A and undergraduate levels. The exercises on each text have been tailored to meet the various assessment objectives laid down in the subject criteria for GCE AS and GCE A Level English Literature, and are explained in such a way that they can easily be selected and fitted into a lesson plan. Given the diversity of ways in which the awarding bodies have devised their specifications to meet these assessment objectives, a wide range of exercises is offered. We've had fun devising the plans, and we hope they'll be fun for you when you come to teach and learn with them.

And if you are neither a teacher nor a student of contemporary literature, but someone reading for your own pleasure? Well, if you've ever wanted someone to introduce you to a novelist's work in a way that will let you trust your own judgement and read more confidently, then this guide is also for you.

Whoever you are, we hope that you will enjoy using these books and that they will send you back to the novels to find new pleasures.

All page references in this text refer to the Vintage edition.

Ian McEwan

Introduction

At the end of Ian McEwan's *The Comfort of Strangers* (1981) a man is murdered. It's a cruel ritualised death, slow, tortured, enjoyed by the perpetrators – a man and a woman who can relate to each other only through a bizarrely sexualised world of shared abuse. There is a witness. The man's girlfriend. And us, of course: you and me – the readers.

The girlfriend, Mary, knows what is happening, what has happened by the end of the novel, but she can't do anything about it because she's been drugged. The perpetrators want her to see, but they don't want her to intervene. It's a scene that takes place over – we have to guess – several hours, but in the print space of the novel it takes up only two and a half pages. More than that, it's a scene that is hardly witnessed. Mary drifts in and out of consciousness. She cannot relate to the sounds, to the images of this obscenity, all too ordinary, to the colours, as the scarlet blood shed in the early evening turns to rust tracks in the sunshine of the morning.

It's a peculiarly modern and modernist trope in literature. The narrative gives us not the centre, but the margin. Something happens, and we are looking away. We are, like Mary (even though she is present), 'altogether elsewhere'. It's a phrase borrowed from a poem by W. H. Auden, a writer whose critical and oblique world view has had great influence on writers of the succeeding generation. But the phrase contains its own contradiction, both for Auden himself and for McEwan's writing.

Over the years since 1975, when McEwan's first book appeared, he has looked unflinchingly at the obsessions, anxieties and events that make up a world in Western culture. The very first story, 'Homemade', in his first collection *First Love, Last Rites* (1975), was about a pubescent boy obsessed with losing his virginity and going about it by raping his little sister. *In Between the Sheets* (1978) includes a story that is the confession of a murderer; *The Cement Garden* (1978) tells how a family of children, desperate to stay together after the deaths of their father and mother, strive to conceal the fact that they have been orphaned by burying their mother's corpse under the patio; *The Comfort of Strangers* (1981) plays on the urban dweller's fear of the unknown; *The Child in Time* (1987) deals with every parent's nightmare of an abducted child; *The Innocent* (1990), set in Berlin, is about spying and distrust, the Cold War and the dismemberment of a city and a body; *Black Dogs* (1992) worries despairingly at relations between men and women, between parents and children, juxtaposed with a new hope for Europe, symbolised by the tearing down of the Berlin Wall; *Enduring Love* (1997) is about obsession, the failure of scientific rationalism, the breakdown of trust; *Amsterdam* (1998) offered early death, betrayal and loneliness; and *Atonement* (2001) gives us false accusation, rape, selfishness and the painful legacy of the Second World War. Even McEwan's libretto for an oratorio, with music by Michael Berkeley and called *Or Shall We Die?* (1983), was based on the script of a documentary on Hiroshima by Jonathan Dimbleby and on the words of two survivors of the nuclear attack. It can sound like a bleak list. And McEwan is still sometimes accused of being 'the master of evil in Eng. Lit.' But that misses the point. We are anxious. If the twentieth century was difficult and dangerous – literally – then it was also a time of serious moral thought and significant philosophy. We may not wish to look directly at scenes of horror. We may actually need to focus on the margins. But that does not mean that we are not looking.

When we began with that short scene from *The Comfort of Strangers*, we said that it only lasts two and a half pages in print. True. But it need last no longer. We have seen, just as Mary saw, and if we do not understand, then the simple act of seeing, of being told what happened, might allow us to begin to understand. This is the role of the intellectual in the face of atrocity. He or she speaks the unspeakable and makes speech itself, not a salve, but a new process. They say what cannot otherwise be spoken. Above all, they say what cannot be spoken by those most qualified to speak – those who have suffered.

In an essay entitled 'Writers, Intellectuals, Teachers' the French literary theorist Roland Barthes says something about the distinction between speech and writing and the paradox of how words on the wind last longer than words on the page: 'Speech is irreversible: a word cannot be *retracted*, except precisely by saying that one retracts it. To cross out is here to add: if I want to erase what I have just said, I cannot do it without showing the eraser itself (I must say: "or rather ..." or, "I expressed myself badly ..."). Paradoxically, it is ephemeral speech that is indelible, not monumental writing. All that one can do in the case of a spoken utterance is to tack on another utterance.'

By speaking about pain we cannot take it away. But we can add to what happened. We can change the story by telling a different story. There is, in any case, never any one story. Only many stories. And by telling those stories, one of the things that McEwan's work does is to change the stories that went before.

If this sounds too overtly moral, it is relevant to McEwan's work because storytelling is the theme that marks his work over and again. Many of his characters, especially his first-person narrators, or those main characters whose point of view dominates a novel, are ... writers. It's no accident. How you tell a story, what it means to tell a story, the perspective, the style, the method, the facts told, the facts left out, the lies, the subterfuge, the drive: all of these minute interests are urgent in his work. But then, after all, they are not so minute, either. The fact is that we only understand the world and our own experience in it by telling a story, or all those many stories.

Connected to this, but in some ways a separate concern, is McEwan's interest in language. It's his vehicle, certainly. But he also knows that it is one that can be abused, used to deceive, to cheat, to deprave. Against this desecration, he sets what he so often calls 'clarity' – precision of expression, the exact term in the right place, the well-judged phrase perfectly balanced to convey what it is designed to say. McEwan says in the interview published in this book that 'clarity' is something he cares about in language far more than what he calls 'music'. It's true that his is not a sonorous style, and yet it does retain a wit and an exactitude that give a similar pleasure. In *Enduring Love* there is a moment when the central character is visiting Soho in London and is worrying about incidents in his life that are making him feel 'contaminated', 'soiled', 'filthy'. Then he steps out into Meard Street. It's the name of a real street, but it's also a joke in French. It's tiny, but it's there, another small balancing word story to help with the larger balancing stories of how to cope with experience – extreme experience in the everyday, and everyday experience in the extraordinary. And one of the things that helps us to know which is which is the ordinary miracle of fiction.

In *Atonement* the main character is a novelist writing a novel. She has, just about, finished that novel by the end of the book.

It will be published after she is dead, and though it is a story about something that really happened to her, she knows that by then she herself will have become – as far as her readers are concerned – no more than a character in a fictional story. She will, as McEwan says, 'only exist within the frame of the novel'. But this wiping out of self in favour of the story is, he says, 'something rooted in the emotional rather than the intellectual'. He goes on, 'I wanted to play with the notion of storytelling as a form of self-justification, of how much courage is involved in telling the truth to oneself.' McEwan, too, will become – is already, of course, in strictly literary theoretical terms – only a character in the story of his fiction. In the meantime his work tries to tell truths about writing, about storytelling, about language, about experience. And that story of a story, might give us – the readers, who are also witnesses – courage to do the same.

Interview with Ian McEwan

Oxford: 21 September 2001

THE CHILD IN TIME

JN: How did you begin *The Child in Time*?

IM: *The Child in Time* was one of those novels that didn't really begin with any clear route map. It had its origins in a number of little scraps, pieces, ideas, enthusiasms. One of them was a recurrent dream, the sort of dream that you only remember that you've had before when it comes again – finally I remembered it and wrote it down. And I should say that dreams have very rarely been a source of inspiration to me, nor am I a great believer in them, despite the plot of the novel. This dream was of myself on a drizzly day walking along a country footpath and coming to a bend in the road and pausing there, with a very powerful premonition that if I walked off to my left I would come to a place ... a pub or a meeting place of some sort, and I would find out something very important about my origins. And it was actually rather a scary dream, and it made me begin to think about how I might write about a character, not quite myself, and what he was doing on this road, and what would happen when he got to this place. So that was one part of it.

Quite separately from that, and at the time I didn't know that these were at all connected, I was reading a rather remarkable book called *Dream Babies* by Christina Hardyment. It's a sort of history of childcare manuals – a most unlikely book. I think I was reading it because someone had given it to me for my birthday, that was about the only reason. I hadn't gone looking for it, it was a piece of complete serendipity, and its subtitle was 'Childcare from Locke to Spock'. What Hardyment was suggesting, among many other things, was that childcare manuals are an extraordinarily accurate way into the spirit of an age. You have the intense regulation of the Victorian notion of breaking a child's will, followed by a rather sentimental child-centred Edwardian view, followed by the rather grisly pseudo-scientific notion of childcare that predominated in the 1920s and '30s, with a lot of input from behaviourists, and then in 1948 . . . Spock.

And this was the early '80s, with what would turn out to be a rather radical and successful government taking control, and we, the children of Spock, were rather surprised by the popularity of this government – not so popular in 1981, but certainly by 1984 – and I thought, 'Well, maybe it's time for another childcare manual.' And I did in fact think of a rather satirical and Swiftian childcare manual that I might write, and I thought, 'No, this is going to be too long and the joke's going to be too sustained'. But I kept little fragments of this.

Then I began to see how these things might fold together. There was my interest in science, which I'd had since my teens, always rather regretting that I hadn't done a science degree at university, fascinated by what I could understand of quantum mechanics and relativity theory, interested generally too in Newtonian mechanics and the history of science, and slowly these things began to fall together.

I had begun the book thinking I was writing a social comedy. Sometime halfway through I began to revise that notion, went back to the beginning, wrote the chapter in which the little girl is lost, and really started again; and by then – because I was anticipating the birth of my first child – I began to have a clear sense that this was a novel that was going to end with a birth, and in fact it ended with a descriptive scene drawn from the birth of two children. By the time I finished in 1986 I had two sons.

JN: Why is it that trauma – and, linked to that, the idea that security is a comforting illusion, but only an illusion – is a focus in so much of your work?

IM: Well, no one, finally, can feel completely secure in the world. There is always an edge of danger, and we're talking on September 21st, 2001, only ten days after the most dramatic illustration of that [the terrorist attack on the World Trade Centre, New York]. Security is what we find mostly in our relationships, but they can't defend us from the outside world.

And I suppose I have been interested more generally in how private fates and public events collide. *The Child in Time* was very much an attempt to write about something quite intimate, like childcare, and something quite public, like a childcare manual. I think the reason I was excited by *Dream Babies* was that it gave me a way in to just that mix of public and private concern. Love is very fragile and difficult to attain, and hard to keep and all the more precious for it. The novel – all novels, not just mine – is extended and extended through time, and with that comes change, difficulty and the exploration of conflict. If we want to simply celebrate love, say, then I think we must turn to lyric poetry. A four hundred page novel celebrating a love affair that never went wrong could be very demanding on the reader.

JN: The novel suggests, especially towards the end, that there's a deeper patterning to time than we're immediately aware of. How did you arrive at that idea?

IM: Well, there any many notions played with in *The Child in Time* that I'm not sure I really hold with, but that were attractive and convenient in an exploration, an investigation of childhood and how it sits within us all our lives, and how in some respects, when we contemplate our whole existence, it seems to be in a perpetual present. That's a very subjective sense of time and childhood, of course, but I was rather intrigued by the way that certain quantum-mechanical versions of time seem to completely undo the standard clock-time sense of it, and I thought that I could forge – with a little bit of creaking and groaning from the subject itself – a connection between this mathematically-based notion of time and all sorts of other versions of it: not only the permanent sense of the whole past living inside your head, but also the way time accelerates in a crisis. Remember, too, that the novel more or less unfolds within the gestation period of a pregnancy. The child is conceived in Chapter Three and the novel then is framed by that sense of impending arrival.

JN: *The Child in Time* has an elaborate formal structure. How much working out of that formal structure might be done before you begin to write?

IM: With a novel like *The Child in Time*, as I said, its beginnings were haphazard. It's impossible to plan the architecture of something unless you know its content, so the structure gets worked out along the way in this kind of novel. I'm very aware of it. It seems to me something that's genuinely operative – that is to say, I think it really does affect the way a reader responds to it. A sense of shape might not be immediately perceived by a reader, but I think the effect on the reader is an added clarity.

I think architecture really makes for clarity, and it's clarity
that I'm most interested in in the sentences too – not princi-
pally music, but precision and a strong visual clarity. So as I
become clearer about what it is I'm going to do, so I make
alterations to the shape of what is going to happen in the
future. Then of course there is the delicious moment of having your first draft down finally, and then you can go back
and make sure that everything conforms to that architectural
sense.

JN: How much re-drafting might you do typically?

IM: Well, everything's changed a great deal with word processing. *The Child in Time* was the first novel I ever wrote on
a word processor. Before that I was never quite settled on a
way of doing drafts. *The Comfort of Strangers* was written in longhand and sent out to be typed. I found that to be very unsatisfactory. *The Cement Garden* I wrote in longhand and typed up
myself – slightly less unsatisfactory, but typewriters I found
were a real problem: a machine seemed very much to inter-
pose in the immediacy of writing by hand.

Word processing, I think, delivered me into a wonderful
virtual space. The chapter that is in the computer, but not yet
printed, has the same – or the equivalent – virtual quality as
an idea in your head that you've not committed to paper yet.
Since working with a word processor, I've been able to do far
more drafts than I otherwise would. So I revise all the time,
I'm constantly going back. It's hard for me to say how many
drafts there were of *The Child in Time*. I revise the previous
day's work first thing in the morning, that's the first combing-
through. When I get four or five thousand words together, a
chapter, two chapters, I do a second ... then I don't look at
them again until I've got the first draft down. I'm only revis-
ing just behind me, as it were, as I go forward.

14

The Child in Time I suppose had three major drafts, with lots and lots of those sorts of local immediate revisions. I do work fairly slowly. I'm not the kind of writer who, in a second draft, is consigning a hundred and twenty pages to the dustbin and then writing another hundred and twenty or twice that. But my drafts will be printed out in double-space: another pleasure and luxury of word processing. I like working through drafts most at night ... A pool of light, a black pen, and I really start attacking it with a sort of freedom, knowing that, again, everything I write here is virtual. More coolly the next morning I might say, 'Well, yes, I'll leave that', or I might accept that change. That's the chance, though, not only to deal with the sentences locally, read them aloud, taste them, test them, but to look at those larger things that you mentioned, such as the formal structure, which is like architecture.

Novels do resemble buildings. A first chapter, a first line is like an entrance hall, a doorway. The reader has to be drawn in – what first meets the eye is important. So I don't use or accept the term architecture merely as a metaphor, I think, again, it's operable, it's something that works on the reader. You're asking the reader to step inside a mental space which has a shape. That's very like someone stepping inside a modern building, going to look at it and deciding whether they like it or not.

ENDURING LOVE

JN: At the beginning of *Enduring Love* you're drawing the reader in. What else are you doing with that opening section?

IM: Well, its narrator is a failed scientist and a successful science journalist, with a particular cast of mind – a highly organised mind – and I wanted immediately to suggest this kind of mind.

It's a chapter that relies heavily on a very disciplined sense of the visual, and of the relationship of the different figures. There are characters converging across a field . . . Joe's way of describing those is in terms of their distance, their points of the compass, there are lots of precise visual details to suggest someone who has got a fairly confident grip on the world, the sort of grip that I would associate with someone who embraces a strong materialist view of it. So the characterisation of Joe was central to that.

Secondly, I'd read that de Clérambault's syndrome – this strange psychotic delusional state – is often triggered by an intense moment. When I started *Enduring Love* I didn't have that intense moment; this opening chapter that people have liked was not written until – I don't know – halfway through the novel, when I found the sort of thing I wanted. But from the point of view of Jed Parry – a lonely man, very much an outsider with his own deep intrapsychic world – to be plunged suddenly into this community of work was, I thought, a way of triggering his particular delusion that Joe loves him.

More broadly, I suppose that I wanted to – cynically, if you like – hook the reader. Again in that architectural sense, this is the first room I wanted the reader in, and I wanted the door locked behind them. And I suppose too that I wanted to suggest, in Joe's way of analysing and describing what's happening, something out of game theory and evolutionary psychology, a Darwinian way of looking at the world. That is, to talk about who lets go first as something that involves morality, involves instinct, involves an adaptationist account of why we are what we are, quite distinct from the deist account that Jed is going to espouse.

JN: And then the third point of view, which you play off against the other two, is Clarissa's as a university teacher who specialises in a Romantic poet, John Keats. Why did you choose that as the third counterpoint?

IM: She just sort of grew. I mean, one doesn't map these things out. I wanted Joe's world to be intact and loving and broadly sympathetic, in order for it to seem all the more threatening that Jed moves into it. I wanted someone both sympathetic and wrong. I wanted in Joe someone who was slightly repellent, but right. It's sometimes quite clear in life that it's not the nicest people who are right. Sometimes someone is dead right, but you don't like them.

I'm aware too that there's a tradition in Western literature that celebrates the heart, the intuition, trusting your feelings. Perhaps it derives a great deal from our Romantic tradition. The scientific, the rational, is often cast into the minds of villains, and I think Mary Shelley might have a lot to answer for in this. But I thought I would like to write a novel that rather celebrated the rational. Not necessarily by making my rational hero too sympathetic, but by celebrating his thought processes. So in Clarissa I wanted someone who was very sympathetic, who had her own sort of enduring love, not only for Keats, but for finding or projecting more letters from Keats and Fanny Brawne – one of the greatest love affairs conducted by letter in literature, I think.

And I wanted the reader to side with Clarissa. There are all kinds of false trails in *Enduring Love*. I wanted the reader to toy with the idea that Joe might be going completely crazy, or maybe even that Joe was Jed. These are games one plays, and withholding information is crucial to this kind of novel writing. But I wanted Clarissa to be wrong. I wanted the police to be wrong. I rather like those plots. I once wrote a movie with Macaulay Culkin in it. It had a similar plot, completely different circumstances, where someone has an understanding of the truth, and none of the other characters – including the reader, including the audience – believe them. I'm sure I'll come back to that. I don't know why it's there, but it's something that I haven't yet played through.

JN: Like *The Child in Time*, *Enduring Love* plays on the idea that communication between two people can be very difficult, even if those two people are close. Why should this be?

IM: I think I can only answer that in terms of the nature of the novel. Clearly misunderstandings occur in life all the time. Not only between people who are very close, but between people who are not close, simply because they don't understand each other. We see this played out at national levels, we see it in sectarian disputes, we see it when marriages come to an end, or love affairs collapse. What is exceptional, I think, about the novel as a form – and here it exerts its superiority over movies, over theatre – is its peculiar ability to get inside minds and to show us the mechanics of misunderstanding, so you can be on both sides of the dispute. You can have unreliable narrators that will draw the reader into the wrong side of a dispute, and then turn it round later. You can be single-minded about it and withhold information, you can be omniscient. But over two or three hundred years we have evolved a literary form that I think is unequalled in its ability to get inside the nature of a misunderstanding. And misunderstandings can stretch from something that is mild and social and comic, to the deepest forms of hatred. Though – and this comes back to the way that three or four or five hundred pages have to take you through a period of time – it cannot really dwell in one moment, so again it can look from all sides at the nature of misunderstanding. So inevitably if you write novels you're going to find yourself writing about – at some level – conflict between people.

ATONEMENT

JN: *Atonement* is partly about guilt. You've said that a novel can look at all sides of a question and it can refuse to take sides. Nevertheless we are encouraged in *Atonement* to take sides, partly because the narrator turns out to have been part of the story, and is therefore partial. What's the significance of the possibility that this 'atonement', this account – the nearest Briony, as a non-believer, can get to 'atonement' – may be inaccurate? Another fantasy?

IM: Part of the intention of *Atonement* was to look at storytelling itself. And to examine the relationship between what is imagined and what is true. It's a novel full of other writers – not only Briony of course, who's stalked, haunted by the figures of Virginia Woolf, Elizabeth Bowen, Rosamond Lehmann, but Robbie too has a relationship, a deep relationship with writing and storytelling.

The danger of an imagination that can't quite see the boundaries of what is real and what is unreal, drawn again from Jane Austen – another writer who is crucial to this novel – plays a part in Briony's sense that her atonement has consisted of a lifetime of writing this novel. She's condemned to write it over and over again. Now she's a dying woman, she has vascular dementia, her mind is emptying, and finally she writes a draft which is different from all the others. She fails, as she sees it, to have the courage of her pessimism, and rewrites the love story so that the lovers survive.

What really then is the truth? Well, as she says, when the novel will finally be published, which can only be after she's dead, she herself will become a character, and no one will be much interested in whether she is real or not, she will only exist within the frame of the novel. So I wanted to play, but play seriously, with something rooted in the emotional rather than the intellectual. I wanted to play with the notion of story-telling as a form of self-justification, of how much courage is involved in telling the truth to oneself. What are the distances between what is real and what is imagined? Catherine Morland, the heroine of Jane Austen's *Northanger Abbey*, was a girl so full of the delights of Gothic fiction that she causes havoc around her when she imagines a perfectly innocent man to be capable of the most terrible things. For many, many years I've been thinking how I might devise a hero or heroine who could echo that process in Catherine Morland, but then go a step further and look at, not the crime, but the process of atonement, and do it through writing – do it through storytelling, I should say.

JN: So Briony's a writer. Joe is a writer. Stephen is a writer. What do you think about being a writer, writing about writers?

IM: I think it could be immensely sterile if that's all it was. I think that I'm always drawn to some kind of balance between a fiction that is self-reflective on its own processes, and one that has a forward impetus too, that will completely accept the given terms of the illusion of fiction. I've never been interested in that kind of fiction that triumphantly declares that art is not life. Only novelists ever think that art is life. Readers never have any problem with it. But I do have an interest in something self-reflective along the way.

JN: A number of novelists born just after the Second World War have written about the experiences of their parents' generation. What are the reverberations of the violence of the Second World War to the generation that grew up in its shadow?

IM: Well, I was born in 1948 and my father was a professional soldier. The war shaped our family life. It was the war that brought my parents together. It was the war that killed my mother's first husband. I grew up in army camps in places in the world in which, again, our presence was to some extent determined by the recent war. And then, more importantly, I suppose, it was the war that set in place the alignments of countries that brought us into the Cold War. It was such a constant presence in my childhood. My father and his friends, as soon as they had a beer in their hand in the evenings, which was every evening, would talk about the war. Wherever they started in their conversation, that's where it would always end. It was a constant presence, and geopolitically it remained a presence.

So as we reached the end of the twentieth century our generation, fiftyish, looked back. The Berlin Wall came down in 1989, and with it came a momentary optimism about a new world order, which rapidly foundered as of last week, so it seemed natural always to return, to focus one's attention on this defining time. Especially when it pushed a contrast on us between our parents' lives and our own. My parents' lives were shaped by the great Depression and the Second World War. I was born in 1948, the beginning of the welfare state. I don't come from either a literary or a wealthy family, but I had access to the most extraordinary education that someone in my social position, thirty years before, would not have been able to take advantage of. It was an unprecedented period of prosperity and relative stability, and there were enormous differences between those generations. As great, I think, actually greater than the kinds of differences that Virginia Woolf and her contemporaries dramatised between themselves and their late-Victorian parents.

JN: You include some highly graphic scenes of violence. We're used to seeing violence in popular culture. What are the differences between artistic and exploitative representations of violence, do you think?

IM: If violence is simply there to excite, then it's merely porno-graphic. I think treating it seriously — which means doing it without sentimentality — you're always going to bring to it a certain quality of investigation, so it's not only the violence you show, you're writing *about* violence. You're showing some-thing that's certainly common in human nature. You're not nec-essarily taking sides, it's not necessary always to produce a moral attitude, but in the greater scheme of things you are bound to place the reader in some form of critical attitude towards the circumstances. There is always a larger intent.

For example, if you're writing about the retreat to Dunkirk, as I do in *Atonement*, you can't avoid the fact that tens of thou-sands of people died in that retreat, and yet we have a rather fond memory of it in the national narrative, and you want to play off something of the sentimentality of the 'miracle' of Dunkirk against the reality for ordinary soldiers as they made their way towards the beaches. Many of the images that I used in the Dunkirk episode I drew from the Bosnian conflict. I used photographs from that to remind myself of how soldiers and civilians, hugely intermingled, would suffer the most appalling consequences.

I talked of sentimentality. I think that is the recurring ele-ment of popular culture's treatment of violence. There are no consequences. Someone gets hit over the head with a bottle and they fall, the camera moves on, the plot moves on. Anyone who's hit on the head with a bottle is likely to suffer a life-time of consequences. Blindness might be one of those, because the visual regions are at the back of the head. In other words, you've got to embrace it, and you've got to make your reader do what Conrad did in his famous Preface to *The Nigger of the Narcissus* (1897), you've got to make your reader *see*. So, when people accuse me of being too graphic in my depic-tions of violence, my response is, 'Well, either you *do* violence, or you sentimentalise it.' If you're going to have it, you've got to show it in all its horror. It's not worth doing it if you're simply going to add it there as a little bit of spice. I'm not interested in that at all.

JN: Do you have a reader in mind as you write?

IM: It's always difficult to answer that question. I suppose it's my most crabby, sceptical self. A rather hard-to-please, ungenerous soul, whose most common remark is 'Come off it!' But it's always a version of myself. I think there's a danger for writers as they get older, and as they become well established, that no one really will tell them anything they don't want to hear.

JN: In what ways do you see your writing developing in the future?

IM: I think I've come to the end of a cycle of novels with *Enduring Love*, which began with *The Child in Time*, included *Black Dogs* and *The Innocent*. Those were novels in which *ideas* were dramatised or played out. They are, among other things, novels of ideas. Both *Amsterdam* and *Atonement* are moving off in another direction. I suppose the emotions perhaps will mean more to me. I think I might, in formal terms, be moving backwards for a little while into the nineteenth century. I spent the summer reading Tolstoy and Chekhov. I'm about to read George Eliot's *Middlemarch*. I think the nineteenth-century novel perhaps brought the form to its point of – or one point of – perfection. I think, in the creation of character, the great nineteenth-century novels are unsurpassed, and I think that I might push forward in my own little projects to make my novels more character-led.

When I got to the end of *Atonement* I felt that Briony was the most complete person I'd ever conjured, and I'd like to do that again and take it further.

The Child in Time

IN CLOSE-UP

Reading guides for

THE CHILD IN TIME

BEFORE YOU BEGIN TO READ . . .
— Read the section on *The Child in Time* from the interview. You will see that McEwan identifies a number of themes and techniques that are present in the novel. These themes include:

- Time, science and art
- Childhood
- Language
- Political manipulation
- Trauma and loss
- Narrative structure.

Other themes and techniques that it may be useful to consider while reading the novel include:

- Relations between men and women
- Child abduction and its effects
- Public policy and individual liberty
- Absence and presence
- Narrative style and genre.

While you are reading *The Child in Time*, *Enduring Love* and *Atonement* in detail it is worth bearing the overall themes listed at the beginning of each reading guide in mind. At the end of each reading guide you will find suggested contexts, which will help you to situate the novel's themes in a wider framework. The reading activities given below are not designed to be followed slavishly. Choose whichever sections most interest you or are most useful for your own purposes. The questions that are set at the end of the chapter plan are to help you relate each individual chapter to the novel as a whole.

Reading activities: detailed analysis

CHAPTER ONE
SECTION 1 (pp. 1-3)

Focus on: openings

SEARCH . . .

— If you are to go on reading a novel, you have to *want* to do that. What is an author likely to want to achieve with the opening of a novel?

— Read the sections in the interview with McEwan that deal with the structure of the novel and the way openings should work. Relate these principles and ideals to the opening of *The Child in Time*.

COMPARE . . .

— Find openings to three novels that contrast in style and approach to the methods adopted by McEwan. You might try Charles Dickens's *A Tale of Two Cities* (1860-1), John Steinbeck's *The Grapes of Wrath* (1939) or George Orwell's *Nineteen Eighty-four* (1949).

— Draw up a list of what the author achieves in those opening pages in terms of establishing tone, viewpoint, characterisation, themes and narrative progression. Then read the opening pages of *The Child in Time* and discuss what this novel achieves in the first three pages. How is the reader drawn in?

Focus on: themes

ANALYSE, WITH A CLOSE READING OF THE CHAPTER EPIGRAPHS . . .

— Each chapter of *The Child in Time* is prefaced by a quotation from a fictitious text, *The Authorised Childcare Handbook*. Read all of these quotations together, and consider the views they put forward about childhood, about men's and women's roles within the family, and about the family's role within the state. Consider also the language through which those views are expressed.

CHAPTER ONE
SECTION 2 (pp. 3–6)

Focus on: language

Lying behind this section is a pattern of contradictions between the language used to describe something and the reality (or how that reality reveals itself to Stephen). Language is manipulated artfully to create a way of seeing or to produce a desired end and the language employed here suggests the possibilities of slipperiness and ambiguity.

ANALYSE VOCABULARY AND WORD CHOICE . . .

— There are many examples in this section of language that obfuscates, that is mealy-mouthed, that dresses reality up to make it appear different. Examples might include: 'It was generally agreed'; 'a desirable citizenry'; 'what should be done to children'; 'Everyone was on a sub-committee'; 'through the influence of his friend'. What does each of these phrases betray about the reality it only partly hides? Why has the reality been 'clothed' with words to make it appear in a different guise?

Focus on: characterisation

EXAMINE LANGUAGE AND IMAGES . . .

— The character of Stephen is developed in this section. Identify the words and images that cluster around Stephen and contrast them with those around Parmenter. What impressions of these two characters are created by these words? What is the effect of the extended conceit of Parmenter depicted as a lizard?

CREATE A PATTERN . . .

— Pick two people from public life, one of whom you broadly admire and one of whom you don't. Write their names at the top of a sheet of paper. Under each name, write a list of words that describe that person to your mind: not just adjectives, but images, symbols, metaphors and any other ideas that come to you. You are describing these people, but also creating them as characters. Consider how they present themselves to your imagination in terms of their appearance, their personality, their moral attitudes, their public career, their private lives, their interests, their special skills, their weaknesses.

— Now consider how you would show these characteristics if you were to put these characters into a novel. Which would you describe explicitly and which would you imply through their ways of behaving? Choose a couple of characteristics for each, then invent and write down a brief situation or a snippet of conversation in which this characteristic is conveyed by the way the character talks and acts, without requiring any commentary from you. If you need inspiration, look again at this section.

31

Focus on: narrative structure

TRACE AND RELATE . . .

— What atmosphere does the narrative establish in 'the gloomy room in Whitehall', with its 'tall window through which, even in midsummer, no sunlight ever passed'?

— Now look ahead to the description of the room on pp. 6–7. What is the effect of the contrasting images of frameworks in the present (weekly structure, window, rectangle, framed, courtyard, framework, outlined, enclosed) with images of the lost time and lost landscape of his memories on that page?

CHAPTER ONE
SECTION 3 (pp. 6–16)

Focus on: narrative structure

CONTRAST AND COMPARE . . .

— Think about the ways in which the novel sets up *contrasts* as the main structural method in this passage.

— To what extent does the narrative employ contrasting tones for the scenes in the past and those set in the narrative present?

— The novel tells the crucial scene of Kate's disappearance as a memory, rather than in the narrative present. What difference does this make?

COMPARE . . .

— Read W. H. Auden's poem 'Musée des Beaux Arts'. Think about how – in both the poem and in this account of the moment of Kate's disappearance – the main event happens on the margins, 'at the periphery of vision' (p. 10). What does this do to your perspective?

CHAPTER ONE
SECTION 4 (pp. 16–21)

Focus on: the theme of social and personal values

SUMMARISE, WITH A CLOSE READING . . .
— How does the account of Mrs Spankey's speech on p. 17, and the way it is delivered, convey a reassuring set of values?

ANALYSE WORD CHOICE AND SOCIAL VALUE . . .
— How does the vocabulary used here imply that these reassurances represent a consciously chosen stance rather than an irrefutable set of truths?

CONSIDER PLOT STRUCTURE AND SOCIAL VALUE . . .
— Read a fairy story. Does the plot carry an implicit message about how to behave or about who gets rewarded in life? How does the story use language to support this view? Can you think of any children's stories that are not essentially reassuring (such as Grimm's fairy tales)?

CREATE THE SCENE . . .
— We are not told anything about the conversation between Stephen and Julie when he explained what had happened in the supermarket. Write out this (absent) section of the novel, either as a dialogue within a novel, or as a drama script. How does Stephen tell this terrible story? How does Julie react – not just to the news, but also to Stephen? Once it is finished, read your dialogue aloud, or perform your script with a partner. What effects are created by the absence of this conversation?

CHAPTER ONE

Looking over Chapter One

QUESTIONS FOR DISCUSSION OR ESSAYS

1.   Discuss how the theme of language – its uses, misuses and limitations – has been developed in Chapter One. In what ways is language seen to create thought, and a view of reality, as well as reflect them?

2.   Consider the ways in which images of spaces, rooms and doors have been used as a metaphor for different states of consciousness in this chapter.

3.   By looking carefully at the language – especially vocabulary and word choice – examine the ways in which the narrative method of the first chapter suggests that the characters' sense of security depends on trusting to illusory beliefs.

4.   Comment on the theme of loss in Chapter One.

5.   Describe the ways in which the novel is given a narrative structure in this first chapter.

6.   By what means, and with what success, has the reader's interest in Stephen Lewis been engaged in the first chapter?

CHAPTER TWO
SECTION 1 (pp. 22–30)

Focus on: characterisation

CRITICALLY EVALUATE . . .
— What impressions do you form of Charles Darke from this section? Identify the words, phrases and images that convey these impressions. What are we told explicitly, and what is left implicit? Analyse how the novel sets about creating situations that will bring out Darke's character. Look for early hints that the successful persona that Darke presents disguises a more complicated, less assured character.

Focus on: narrative point of view

ADAPT AND TRANSFORM . . .
— Rewrite an account of Stephen's meeting with Darke in the restaurant, placing Darke's view at the centre of the narrative and indicating his reactions to Stephen and his impressions of his own performance. Compare the effects created by the two points of view.

CHAPTER TWO
SECTION 2 (pp. 30–2)

Focus on: the theme of time

COMPARE AND CONTRAST . . .
— Look at the slightly surreal account of the incidents that lead up to a nuclear stand-off between Russia and the United States. The contrast between the inconsequential, local origins of the stand-off and its potentially worldwide consequences is

35

emphasised: a quick proliferation leads from starting point to unpredictable result. This is one instance of many in the novel of events leading through ever-proliferating branches to unforeseeable consequences.

— Reread pp. 8–11 and identify some moments from which the events leading up to Kate's disappearance could be said to spring. How does the narrative emphasise these? Note how the act of reviewing past events as an image of expanding choices allows one to see a pattern in events that may have appeared chaotic at the time. Now read McEwan's comments on the idea of a pattern underlying the shaping of events, in the interview on pps. 13–14. How do his ideas relate to what happens in this novel?

CHAPTER TWO
SECTION 3 (pp. 32–5)

Focus on: characterisation

ANALYSE WORD CHOICE AND REPRESENTATION . . .
— Think about the language used by Darke on pp. 33–5 and the language used about him. How does this language affect his characterisation, and how does it suggest an ironic view of his commitment and authenticity?

Focus on: language

SEARCH . . .
— Look in the newspapers for coverage of a recent political event, and study what a number of politicians or political spokespeople are quoted to have said in response. Compare their stated views with one other and with the reportage of the event, and look for instances of eloquent deceitfulness.

Focus on: the theme of public policy and individual liberty

DISCUSS . . .
— What implicit commentary is made in this section about the personal qualities that lead to success in the political arena? Are they valid, in your opinion? Write an essay on the topic 'Good people do not make good politicians'. Make sure you clarify what it is that you mean by 'good' in each case.

CHAPTER TWO
SECTION 4 (pp. 36–8)

Focus on: characterisation

CONTRAST . . .
— Analyse the narrative techniques used to convey an impression that Darke has changed since the incidents portrayed earlier in Chapter Two.

CHAPTER TWO
SECTION 5 (pp. 38–40)

Focus on: the theme of time, science and art

COMPARE . . .
— Read the short story *The Time Machine* (1895) by H. G. Wells. How appropriate is fiction as a form for exploring scientific theory? Both writers must somehow explain scientific theory in their narrative: what techniques do they use?

CHAPTER TWO
SECTION 6 (pp. 41–4)

Focus on: the theme of men and women

PRESENT . . .

— What are your impressions of the character of Thelma so far in the novel? In what ways does she behave according to conventional gender roles, and in what ways does she challenge them? Consider these questions, then have a debate on the motion 'This House believes that it is really women who wield most power in our society'.

DISCUSS . . .

— Having finished the chapter, refer back to the quotation from the fictional *Authorised Childcare Handbook* that provided its epigraph (p. 22). In what ways is the quotation relevant to the themes of the chapter?

CHAPTER TWO

Looking over Chapter Two

QUESTIONS FOR DISCUSSION OR ESSAYS

1. Consider how this chapter has developed the following themes:

- Gender roles, and whether these are based primarily on innate differences or on learned prejudices
- The significance of childhood experience
- The ways in which events eclipse a character's intentions and shape a character's disposition
- Time, viewed scientifically and viewed subjectively.

CHAPTER THREE
SECTION I (pp. 45-8)

Focus on: the themes of time and childhood

RECALL AND RELATE . . .

— The epigraph refers to the separations that come between (in the double senses of 'occur between' and 'create a barrier between') childhood and adulthood. Note the developing theme of characters seeing their childhood as a lost part of themselves (in the double senses of 'given up' and 'unlocatable') and feeling a need to find and reconnect with their childhood selves.

— Can you point to a moment in your own childhood or early youth where you can distinguish between your idea of yourself as a child and your idea of yourself as a grown person? What triggered this moment? Was it a large event? Or something relatively insignificant in the eyes of an observer? How might your own experience connect with the images of childhood and memory set out in *The Child in Time*?

TRACE AND ANALYSE . . .

— Look back at the episode about Stephen's memory of being with his parents by the sea on bicycles in the previous chapter (p. 43). It seemed inconsequential there, but it becomes relevant here. A striking aspect of McEwan's work is its tight formal structure: every detail serves a purpose in a wider picture, although the reader must often wait to see how. What does this formal narrative technique do to the reader's experience of reading the novel? In what ways does McEwan imply that Stephen's journey to see his wife is a metaphor for a journey through time? Within this metaphor, what significance do Julie's inadequate and smudged directions take on? In what ways does the opening up of the vista affect Stephen's mood,

39

and what significance does this have as a metaphor for points of view on life? How does this moment relate to the novel as a whole?

CHAPTER THREE
SECTION 2 (pp. 48–51)

Focus on: the theme of men and women

IDENTIFY THE VOCABULARY . . .

— McEwan's writing is valued for the accuracy with which he observes and delineates emotional states. What are the most poignant details of this portrayal of the failure of Stephen and Julie's relationship, in your opinion? Identify all the abstract nouns that are used in this section, up to 'buried beyond their reach', and then identify all the concrete imagery that is used. In what different ways do these two sets of words convey the sense of Stephen and Julie's estrangement?

ADAPT AND ANALYSE . . .

— Reread the account of Julie's attitude to 'destiny' (from 'She was not beyond confusion . . .' to '. . . fulfil one's destiny') and select three key words. Write a brief account of Julie's attitudes to these concepts, as you understand them from this passage; then write an account of your own attitudes to them.

PRESENT . . .

The final two paragraphs of this section put forward Stephen's views on essential differences between men and women. This passage is relevant to a central theme of the novel that will be developed through subsequent events.

— If you are working in a mixed group, separate into male-female pairs. Both members of the pairings should prepare ten questions about the attitudes of the other sex to a range of issues, such as those mentioned in this section of the novel. The two partners in each pair then take it in turns to interview one another about these issues. After the interviews are all over, the group should discuss whether the opinions expressed seemed to support the view that men and women are 'essentially the same', or Stephen's view that they have 'many distinguishing features'.

CHAPTER THREE
SECTION 3 (pp. 51–7)

Focus on: narrative structure

CONSIDER NARRATIVE TECHNIQUE . . .
— Stephen finds himself inhabiting a 'delicate reconstruction of another time' (p. 53). This passage is minutely observed in realistic detail, but is also surreal, and the reader is likely to be confused at first. Where have the black bikes figured previously? What is the 'decision' that they ponder – 'a beckoning or a dismissal' – likely to concern? What effects are created by the narrative strategy of incomplete revelation?

Focus on: the theme of time

DISCUSS . . .
— Consider the ideas that McEwan's narrative is implying in this section about memory, about time and about a collective consciousness. In what ways does this passage seem to bear out Thelma's claim that a 'scientific revolution, no, an intellectual revolution, an emotional, sensual explosion, a fabulous story [is] just beginning to unfold for us . . . Matter, time, space, forces [are] all beautiful and intricate illusions' (p. 40)?

41

CHAPTER THREE
SECTION 4 (pp. 57–61)

Focus on: narrative structure

ANALYSE AND COMPARE . . .
Stephen is aware of standing at a metaphorical fork in his path:
two lives, both unknown, stretch out before him. A present
decision will determine which road he takes, and which will
remain for ever the road not taken.
— Compare the passage (from 'You're looking very beautiful
. . .' [p. 59] to '. . . the desire to belong' [p. 60]) with that in the
first chapter on pp. 8–9 beginning 'He took Julie some tea . . .'
to '. . . through the front door.' How did Stephen make a decision the previous time? Note that this time Stephen makes his
choice 'without deliberation and with an immediacy which felt
both wise and abandoned'. In what ways does McEwan suggest parallels between the two moments and an underlying pattern to events? What does the phrase 'a line of argument'
suggest (consider the connotations of both the words 'line'
and 'argument') in the context of this suggested pattern?

CONSIDER VOCABULARY AND EMOTION . . .
— Analyse the language that is used to describe Stephen and
Julie making love. How do the images and words used connect
with images and words employed earlier (or later) in the novel?

CHAPTER THREE
SECTION 5 (pp. 62–4)

Focus on: language

EXAMINE WORD CHOICE . . .

— The playwright Harold Pinter once claimed that speech is 'a stratagem to cover nakedness'. Analyse the ways in which Stephen and Julie's conversation after having sex acts as just such a stratagem.

CHAPTER THREE

Looking over Chapter Three

QUESTIONS FOR DISCUSSION OR ESSAYS

1. Analyse the ways in which open communication is seen to be difficult (or impossible) between Stephen and Julie in this chapter.

2. What are McEwan's distinguishing qualities as a novelist, based on your reading so far of *The Child in Time*?

3. McEwan is said to be a writer who looks at experience with brilliance and extraordinary intensity. Discuss the technical literary ways in which he creates these effects.

4. Discuss McEwan's use of images of home, enclosure and belonging in this chapter.

5. 'McEwan is masterful at conveying precisely how people feel.' Based on your reading so far, do you agree?

CHAPTER FOUR
SECTION I (pp. 65–71)

Focus on: the theme of childhood

We learn more about Stephen's own childhood, and we see the significance of these childhood experiences in his memory, as we are told about a 'five-year idyll' in North Africa, followed by the separation from that idyll into a harsher world when he went to boarding school, back in England.

SEARCH . . .

— Look up the word 'idyll'. What does it mean? It evokes the tradition of literary pastoral, to which this passage is indebted. What can you find out from a glossary of literary terms about pastoral, and the yearnings for lost innocence that it displays?

— Read the account of Adam and Eve in the Garden of Eden, and their banishment, in the Old Testament, Genesis, Chapters 2 and 3. What parallels can you find with the account of Stephen's childhood idyll and his first separations from it?

ANALYSE . . .

— 'It was a secure and ordered world, hierarchical and caring.' Which of Stephen's memories convey these particular aspects of his childhood in Africa? In what ways does North Africa represent a world culturally far removed from England?

— Does the North African passage convey successfully to you the qualities of childhood experience? If so, how? What place does language occupy in Stephen's memories? How are belonging and unity with the physical world emphasised? What images does McEwan use to indicate Stephen's separation from this childhood world?

44

— Consider the portrayal of the adults in this section. Analyse how Stephen's mother and father appear in his memory. In what ways does the adult world seem both separate from, and a threat to, his childhood idyll? What is the significance of the fact that both Stephen's mother and the old lady on the plane cry at the moment he leaves his childhood behind? Who are they crying for?

CHAPTER FOUR
SECTION 2 (pp. 71–82)

Focus on: the theme of the use and abuse of language

The 'ape-like man' makes a case for the way language breaks a child's sense of harmony with the created world, and forces a premature self-awareness that divorces a person from his unselfconscious childhood self (note the parallel with the Tree of Knowledge that makes Adam and Eve self-conscious). This speech forms a link between the theme of how language can be used and abused and the theme of the loss of childhood. You may be noticing by now the intricacy with which McEwan links all his themes. The man is treated like a crank, but his theory will be supported by what Darke is about to do. McEwan never tells his readers explicitly what to think of his characters, but the novel has an implied set of values that guide our responses in a covert way.

DISCUSS . . .
— To place 'the ape-like man' in the context of the novel's values, compare his use of language with Darke's earlier use on pp. 34–5 (from 'He was a barrage-of-words man . . .' to '. . . the two men laughed into their drinks'). Now contrast it

45

with Stephen's reply, which he argues 'like a politician, a Government Minister', and 'passionately, seemingly innocent of self-interest' (p. 77), an impression that is quickly exposed as sham. Assess the validity of the claim that '*The Child in Time* equates language with power, deceitfulness and corruption'.

TRACE AND EXAMINE . . .
— Underline all of the statements by 'the ape-like man' that have a relevance to Stephen's memories of childhood that precede it. In what ways do Stephen's experiences seem to support the man's thesis?

CONSIDER . . .
— In the context of the views he advocates, what effects are suggested by the description of the man as 'ape-like'? What is the effect of his name – and his status as a professor – being withheld until the end of the section? What do his reactions to the Prime Minister's entry, his unselfconscious violation of protocol and his position standing opposite the Prime Minister suggest about the values and attitudes he symbolises, in contrast to those of the people around him?
— In what ways does the narrative employ satire to ridicule the members of the committee? Notice that Brody escapes the satire, yet the other committee members have not taken him seriously. What is implied about their inability to see clearly? In contrast, note Brody's steady 'gaze'.
— What effects are created by the narrative trick of withholding from us knowledge of the Prime Minister's gender?

CHAPTER FOUR
SECTION 3 (pp. 82–9)

Focus on: the theme of children and parents

ACCOUNT FOR . . .
— Why, in your opinion, has Stephen gone to see his parents?
— Consider the roles that Stephen's parents have adopted in their marriage. What do these indicate about their shared life?
— Study the portrayal of Stephen's father. It borders on caricature. What can you glean about his view of the world from what he says about Stephen's committee work? To what extent are his views individual, and to what extent are they commonplace or received?

CONSIDER . . .
— 'It was typical of what bound the three of them that they had never been able to grieve Kate together (p. 86).' What does this say about Stephen's relationship with his parents? What other signs are there in this section that suggest that open communication between them is difficult?

ASK YOURSELF . . .
— In your opinion, is it true that 'parents are strangers to their children'? Ask why this is so, if you think it is. How do your own ideas on this relate to McEwan's novel as a whole?

Focus on: the sense of place

OUTLINE AND ANALYSE . . .
— Illustrate and explain the depiction of Stephen's parents' house. What is the significance of the fact that they have lived all their married lives in 'borrowed' houses, until this one? The knick-knacks symbolise their travels, and by implication their

shared lives. How individual an impression of their life is conveyed by these 'cutely represented' symbols (p. 85)?

CHAPTER FOUR

Looking over Chapter Four

QUESTIONS FOR DISCUSSION OR ESSAYS

1. *The Child in Time* exhibits an intricate formal structure.
What is it about the way that literature can give shape to
experience that readers find so satisfying? You might like to
look at the sections in the interview with McEwan where he
talks about the 'shape' and 'architecture' of the novel – any
novel.

2. Political satire has a rich tradition in literature. Read Part
I, 'A Voyage to Lilliput', of Jonathan Swift's *Gulliver's Travels*
(1726). In what ways is Swift's satire on the court of Queen
Anne echoed in McEwan's picture of contemporary politics in
The Child in Time?

3. Consider the validity of the claim that the real subject of
this novel is not the little girl Stephen lost in the supermarket,
but the little boy that he lost in himself.

CHAPTER FIVE
SECTION 1 (pp. 90–8)

Focus on: the theme of time

INTERPRET AND JUSTIFY FROM YOUR OWN EXPERIENCE . . .
— '. . . the rapidity of events was accompanied by the slowing of time' (p. 91). In what sense can time be said to 'slow' in a crisis? Is this subjective experience of time's relative speed an illusion?

DESCRIBE . . .
— Does this scene recall any experiences you may have had when time seemed to change speed? If so, try to describe what happened.

EXAMINE AND JUSTIFY . . .
— The narrative tells us that, had Julie been there, she and Stephen would have been 'curious to understand what it must mean, what significance it had for their future' (p. 92). Do you believe that experiences – even ones that are the result of accident – 'mean' something, or are they merely chance occurrences? (Note that this scene will in fact have a parallel in an important moment in Stephen and Julie's lives later on. Look out for it.)

DISCUSS AND ANALYSE . . .
— Consider the significance of 'points of view' in this section.

49

CHAPTER FIVE
SECTION 2 (pp. 98–112)

Focus on: the themes of time and memory

DEFINE AND RELATE . . .

— 'Stephen thought that if he could do everything with the intensity and abandonment with which he had once helped Kate to build her castle, he would be a happy man of extraordinary powers' (p. 104). Compare this thought – coloured by Stephen's nostalgic memories of Kate – with the experience of being 'engrossed, fully in the moment' (p. 108), when he climbs the tree. What qualities does this experience have? How do they relate to the themes of the novel as a whole?

LIST, CONNECT AND ANALYSE . . .

— Stephen and Charles drink lemonade from the bottle. Stephen's first book was called *Lemonade*. Look for other moments in the novel where characters drink – wine, beer, champagne – from the bottle and consider their significance. Are they celebrations? If so, of what?

COMPARE . . .

— Read J. M. Barrie's *Peter Pan* (1904), Robert Louis Stevenson's *Treasure Island* (1883), R. M. Ballantyne's *The Coral Island* (1857), William Golding's *The Lord of the Flies* (1954) or Susan Hill's *I'm the King of the Castle* (1970). What elements of boys' adventure stories do any of these share with the tale of Charles Darke's own private adventure? In what ways do they differ?

CHAPTER FIVE
SECTIONS 3 AND 4 (pp. 113–20)

Focus on: the themes of science, art, time, men and women

DISCRIMINATE . . .

— What theoretical ideas about time have been hinted at in the novel so far?

— Thelma says, '. . . when [science] could begin to take subjective experience into account, then the clever boy was on his way to becoming a wise woman' (p. 118). What does she mean?

— How does Thelma's argument reflect on the differences between male and female roles as depicted in the ways that Stephen and Julie (or Charles and Thelma, or Stephen's mother and father) respond to events in the novel?

COMPARE . . .

— The quotation on p. 116 is from 'Burnt Norton', the first part of T. S. Eliot's long poem *Four Quartets* (1944). The poem goes on, 'If all time is eternally present / All time is unredeemable'. Read *Four Quartets* and consider how Eliot's ideas are picked up and reinterpreted in *The Child in Time*.

CHAPTER FIVE

Looking over Chapter Five

QUESTIONS FOR DISCUSSION OR ESSAYS

1. 'Innocence is much harder to achieve than experience.' Consider *The Child in Time* in the light of this comment.

2.. Discuss the techniques that McEwan uses to convey the immediacy of experience.

3.   How do images of the natural world figure in this novel?

4.   Consider the development of Darke's characterisation in this chapter.

5.   'Novels are not the place for scientific theorising.' Discuss.

6.   *The Child in Time* has been described as 'spooky' by the critic Jonathan Raban. Account for that impression.

7.   Assess the validity of the claim that *The Child in Time* presents the human experience as one that is essentially lonely.

CHAPTER SIX
SECTION I (pp. 121–9)

Focus on: the theme of loss

DISCUSS . . .
— This section focuses on Stephen's thoughts about Kate at the time of her sixth birthday. In what ways might it be harder to grieve for a child who is lost, but (presumably) still living, than for a child who has died? Pick out key passages to show how Kate's living presence-in-absence informs the whole novel.

INTERPRET . . .
— Stephen buys a walkie-talkie for Kate. What might this particular present symbolise?
— In what sense did Stephen's inner life stop when he lost Kate?

CHAPTER SIX
SECTION 2 (pp. 129–31)

Focus on: language and communication

CONSIDER . . .
— Telephones offer ease of communication, but they also emphasise separation. What does it suggest that this stilted telephone conversation follows immediately on from Stephen's yearning to communicate with Kate?

ILLUSTRATE AND ANALYSE . . .
Find another passage in *The Child in Time* where a character has only a limited means of communication at hand and yet goes on with the attempt. (The letters that Joe composes on pp. 94 and 95 might be examples.) How successful (or otherwise) are those attempts?

CHAPTER SIX
SECTION 3 (pp. 131–7)

Focus on: narrative structure

ANALYSE VOCABULARY . . .
— 'To have a destination, a place where you were expected, a shred of identity, was such a relief after a month of game shows and scotch' (p. 132). Think about the connotations of the words 'destination', 'place' and 'identity'. Look up alternative words for these in a thesaurus. Make a list of which words mean the same and which have subtly different meanings.

EXPLAIN . . .
— Earlier on, Stephen had remarked to Thelma that 'reality'

53

was constructing models to account for one's observations. How do his imagined speeches to Julie illustrate this claim? How does this succession of speeches help shape the novel?

CONTRAST . . .

— The passage in which Stephen thinks of Julie in his imagination echoes his thoughts about Kate: both now seem out of reach. Compare this description of Julie with your own impressions of her so far.

CHAPTER SIX
SECTION 4 (pp. 137–52)

Focus on: narrative and allusion

RELATE . . .

— The children in the playground are singing about sickness, death and healing. There is a suggestive link between this song, Stephen's state of mind and the wider themes of the novel, though there is no surface logic in this link. What is the point of passing references like this to central themes? Can you find other examples?

— Think over as many children's playground songs or games as you can remember or find out about. What are their themes? How many of them deal with sickness and death?

Focus on: the theme of men and women

DISCRIMINATE AND ASSESS . . .

— For a few moments, Stephen's resolve to find Kate gains new strength. Look back to the argument he rehearsed in his head to convince Julie that her reaction to Kate's loss had been 'weak': 'He had gone out searching for their daughter while she sat at home. When he had failed to find her, Julie had blamed him and left, her head full of cant about the proper way to mourn . . . Had he found Kate, then his methods would never have been in doubt' (p. 134). Here it seems as if Stephen's 'methods' are about to be justified. But the hope is short-lived. The novel is beginning to suggest that Julie's decision to accept Kate's loss, to live with the grief and to let it take its course was not weak, but wise.

— Stephen's point of view is skewed by his inability to let go of Kate (think back to his present-buying). Within the terms of the novel, how far is his reaction portrayed as typically 'male', and Julie's as typically 'female'?

DEFINE . . .
— Bearing the above ideas in mind, what is the relevance of the repeated references to perspective as Stephen sits drawing in the classroom?
— McEwan puts in one detail that tells us that the girl Stephen has seized on definitely cannot be Kate, some time before Stephen himself accepts this. Which is the detail? In what ways is it clear that Stephen's mind is playing 'tricks' on him because he wants the girl to be Kate?

CHAPTER SIX
SECTION 5 (pp. 152–4)

Focus on: development of character

ANALYSE . . .
— In a sense Stephen needed to make the mistake he makes at the school. Now he feels 'purged' (p. 152). Of what? How has his attitude to the assistant secretary changed since the first telephone call?

CHAPTER SIX

Looking over Chapter Six

QUESTIONS FOR DISCUSSION OR ESSAYS

1. 'It is our emotions that inform our world view. Our thoughts merely justify the emotions.' Discuss this claim with reference to Chapter Six, or to the novel as a whole.

2. How are the themes of holding on to and letting go of the past developed in Chapter Six of *The Child in Time*?

3. In the previous chapter Stephen had wished that he could achieve the 'true maturity' of a child at play, absorbed in the moment. In what ways do we see that Stephen is absorbed in every other moment *but* the present in this chapter?

4. Consider the ways in which McEwan employs metaphors in *The Child in Time,* and assess their effectiveness.

5. 'Art is ordered. Life isn't. When a writer gives shape to life he is guilty of deliberate misrepresentation.' Discuss.

CHAPTER SEVEN
SECTION I (pp. 155–64)

Focus on: language

EXAMINE YOUR OWN RESPONSE . . .
— To what extent do you agree with the quotation from the *Handbook* that prefaces this chapter?

CONSIDER TERMS AND PHRASES . . .

— What impression do you get in the first two paragraphs of the sub-committee's report? Pick out the four most telling phrases, and say what they suggest about it.

— Read the tennis coach's criticisms about Stephen's playing as if they were about his attitude to the 'game' of life, not tennis. How might they fit this metaphorical interpretation?

— 'The grown ups know best' (p. 163), says Morley of the government's attitude towards the sub-committee that it appointed, which is revealed as dismissive, manipulative and dishonest. Look for details in the quotations from the *Handbook*, in this section and at the heading of each chapter, that betray a similar set of attitudes towards children.

CHAPTER SEVEN
SECTION 2 (pp. 164–6)

Focus on: the theme of men and women

DISCUSS . . .

— 'It's the Air Force training. If it's untidy or doesn't fit, throw it out' (p. 166). Discuss how this comment on Stephen's father's world view fits into the theme of contrasting male and female attitudes to life, as they are worked out in the novel as a whole.

CHAPTER SEVEN
SECTION 3 (pp. 166–77)

Focus on: point of view and change

ANALYSE . . .

— Mrs Lewis tells her own story about how she met and married Stephen's father. This account of her past is the first section of the novel to describe events from a point of view other than Stephen's. In what ways does it offer a corroboration of his experiences? How might this different point of view help to reflect Stephen's decreasingly isolated position?

— 'The past is a foreign country: they do things differently there,' writes L. P. Hartley in the Prologue to *The Go-Between* (1953). In what ways does Mrs Lewis's account of her own past suggest a different set of social values and attitudes from Stephen's? Single out five details that convey these social values as they applied in the period immediately after the Second World War.

RESEARCH . . .

— Interview someone who was already an adult in 1945. Ask about the ways in which social attitudes have changed since that time, particularly in relation to class, gender roles and marriage. How do these real accounts square with the fictional account of these attitudes as depicted in *The Child in Time?*

Focus on: the theme of men and women

COMPARE . . .

— Look at the description of Mrs Lewis's first impressions of her future husband and compare it with the description of the way Gertrude Coppard reacts to Walter Morel in D. H. Lawrence's

Sons and Lovers (1913), Chapter One, from 'When she was twenty-three years old . . .' to '. . . had crystallised out hard as rock'. What masculine characteristics or qualities attract the two women in these accounts? And how successfully do the two writers convey the two women's early disappointments in their relationships?

DISCUSS . . .
— 'they still had to break into speech, raise the difficult subject, tortuously reason it through with lies and false emotion and pretensions to logic before they could attain the conclusion she had already accepted' (p. 174). Discuss the ways in which honest communication is portrayed as impossible in the situation that Claire and Douglas find themselves in.

CONTRAST . . .
— Compare and contrast Claire's and Douglas's reactions to her pregnancy. How do they use language differently here? How do their different reactions fit into the novel's portrayal of the discrepancy between typically male and typically female attitudes?

Focus on: the theme of time

CONSIDER THE SYMBOL . . .
— What do you make of the fact that it is a clock – not any other object – that Douglas was dissatisfied with? What might it suggest that Stephen's mother's maiden name is 'Temperly' (p. 166)?
— What is the significance of the fact that the pub is called 'The Bell' (p. 53)?

COMPARE . . .
— Look back at Thelma's comments in Chapter Five on new scientific theories about the nature of time: '. . . whatever time

is, the common-sense, everyday version of it as linear, regular, absolute, marching from left to right, from the past through the present to the future, is either nonsense or a tiny fraction of the truth' (p. 116); 'In relativity theory time is dependent on the speed of the observer. What are simultaneous events to one person can appear in sequence to another' (p. 116); 'Different kinds of time, not simply the linear, sequential time of commonsense, could be projected through consciousness ...' (p. 118). How does this account support the idea that Mrs Lewis's and Stephen's experiences – decades apart – of the same event are literally possible?

CONSIDER YOUR OWN REACTION . . .

— The moment when Mrs Lewis mentions the boy's face at the window takes the novel's treatment of time on to a new level: until this point, all references to how characters experience time have been couched in terms of the subjectivity of experience. Now the narrative asks us to accept that the past and the present can co-exist. Does this strain credulity?

— Why do you suppose that McEwan has placed Mrs Lewis's account of her memories at this point in the narrative?

COMPARE . . .

Read Volume III, Chapter IX of Charlotte Brontë's *Jane Eyre* (1847), where Jane, in a moment of high emotional tension, seems to hear the disembodied voice of her lover calling to her. He later tells how he too heard her mysterious reply. Compare the treatment of this 'supernatural' or inexplicable event with the treatment of the similar 'out of time' experience in *The Child in Time*. How explicit is each novel in coming to practical conclusions about what has happened? Are either of the events explicable only because they take place in fiction? How satisfying (or otherwise) to the reader's sensibility is the delineation of such mysterious happenings?

CHAPTER SEVEN
SECTION 4 (pp. 177–8)

Focus on: the theme of communication

ANALYSE . . .

— 'There was no need for discussion' (p. 177). Why? This is the first time in the novel that silence between two characters has not been a sign of their inability to communicate. In what ways has Stephen's view of his parents developed since his visit in Chapter Four?

— To Stephen's father, the present is a foreign country. What details in Mrs Lewis's account of their experiences just after the war help to explain why Mr Lewis feels out of place in the contemporary world?

CHAPTER SEVEN

Looking over Chapter Seven

QUESTIONS FOR DISCUSSION OR ESSAYS

1. How are the themes of connection and isolation developed in Chapter Seven?

2. Discuss the ways in which Stephen has changed since the start of Chapter Six, and analyse why he has changed.

3. *The Child in Time* has been described as 'intellectually playful'. Consider how and why this description might fit.

4. 'Men and women, men and women. It will never work' (Erica Jong). Discuss the ways in which the portrayals of relationships between men and women in *The Child in Time* refute or support this view.

CHAPTER EIGHT
SECTION I (pp. 179–92)

Focus on: the theme of childhood

CRITICALLY EVALUATE . . .
— Do the phrases describing childhood as 'a physically and mentally incapacitating condition, distorting emotions, perceptions and reason', extracted from *The Authorised Childcare Handbook* and quoted in the epigraph (p. 179), more accurately describe the novel's picture of childhood or of adulthood?

Focus on: the theme of public policy and individual liberty

ANALYSE THE VOCABULARY . . .
— The account of press and politicians' reactions and counter-reactions to the *Handbook* highlights the theme of truth versus rhetoric. Find examples of ironic words and phrases, statements and stances that point to the distance between the two in public debate.

DISCUSS . . .
— 'Complicated channels ran between truth and lying; in public life the adept survivors navigated with sure instincts while retaining a large measure of dignity . . . Wasn't the interior life much the same?' (p. 182). Consider whether the rules that govern truth and lying in public life are much the same as those that govern truth and lying in the privacy of one's inner life. Can you argue that the novel as a whole comes down on one side or the other?

COMMENT ON . . .
— The Prime Minister's plaintive confidences to Stephen present an ironic slant based on the gap between the Prime Minister's

public and private personae. What are your impressions from this conversation of the private person behind the Prime Ministerial persona? In what ways is this split between the public and private face explored in other places in the novel as a whole?

Focus on: language

COMPARE . . .
— The Prime Minister's obsessive trailing of Darke foreshadows a much more extreme form of obsessive and deluded love in McEwan's later novel *Enduring Love*. Read Chapter Eleven of that novel, where Jed Parry's delusional system of thought is set out. How does Parry appropriate the language of relationships to prop up an insane world view? Does this bear any resemblance to the way that the Prime Minister appropriates the clichéd justifications for adultery?

CHAPTER EIGHT
SECTION 2 (pp. 192–4)

Focus on: the theme of social responsibility

DISTINGUISH AND EVALUATE VOCABULARY . . .
— In the description of the beggars, what does the expression 'the sifting would begin again' mean (p. 193)? What does 'sifting' usually mean, and what is the effect of the word in this context?

SEARCH AND ANALYSE . . .
— On both occasions that he sees a beggar girl, Stephen gives her something. The first occasion occurs in Chapter One on pp. 2–3. Compare the significance of the gifts and the descriptions of each episode.

CHAPTER EIGHT
SECTION 3 (pp. 194–200)

Focus on: the theme of time and change

RELATE AND ANALYSE . . .

— 'Now he ran the house and, according to his wife, loved the work. And she had discovered a new life' (p. 194). Again, an incidental detail articulates a major theme. Think back to the ways in which Stephen's parents have always been constrained by social conventions and gender roles. Now think of the ways in which Stephen has discovered a renewed interest in life. How has this theme of time and change been developed across the novel as a whole?

Focus on: narrative structure

DISTINGUISH TONE AND GENRE . . .

— Read the passage from 'He arrived at the small clearing . . .' (p. 198), to the end of this section. Discuss the ways in which this passage mixes grim naturalism with symbolism, pathos and farce.

CHAPTER EIGHT
SECTION 4 (pp. 200–6)

Focus on: the theme of childhood and narrative structure

CONTRAST AND COMMENT ON . . .

— Given the intricacy with which *The Child in Time* is structured, one would be surprised if McEwan did not tie up all the loose ends. Thelma's explanation of Charles's state of mind brings ideas about the place of childhood to a conclusion. What is the impact of the revelation that *The Authorised Childcare*

Handbook was the result of a partnership between Darke and the Prime Minister? Consider the proleptic ironies that emerge once we know that this book – an exposition of traditional family values, the purpose of which was to influence how a whole nation of parents relate to their children – was the fruit of a union between these two childless and emotionally stultified characters. What new (and rather sinister) connotations arrive from the contrivance of depicting the Prime Minister as a nation's parent of unknown gender?

CHAPTER EIGHT

Looking over Chapter Eight

QUESTIONS FOR ESSAYS OR DISCUSSION

1. Discuss the presentation of politics in this chapter.

2. Consider Stephen's role in Thelma and Charles Darke's relationship, with particular focus on this chapter.

3. 'I have to say that Charles's case was just an extreme form of a general problem' (p. 205). To what extent are Darke's faults and contradictions also evident in other characters in *The Child in Time*?

CHAPTER NINE
SECTION I (pp. 207–13)

Focus on: the theme of childhood

INTERPRET AND CREATE . . .

The mercantile language of the epigraph from *The Authorised Childcare Handbook* takes on an ironic significance following

Thelma's claim that Darke was unable to bring his qualities as a child into his public life. The novel has implied that children are indeed a resource: in the sense that, for each of us, our childish qualities are a powerful emotional resource, if we will allow them to be.

— Look back at the passage from Chapter Three about Stephen's memories of discussing trains with his father: 'Stephen marvelled then at the intricate relation of things, the knowingness of the inanimate, the deep symmetry which conspired to narrow the rail's gauge precisely in keeping with the train's diminishment; no matter how fast it rushed, the rails were always ready' (p. 47). This description captures a child's naïve incomprehension about the physical world; an adult would probably want to correct the child's delusion that the rails diminish with distance. But, as a metaphor for events in the novel, by implication it also describes a childish wisdom that most adults, in their attachment to rationality, have forgotten.

— Think of any examples you can where a child has uttered words in all innocence that actually – from a knowing adult perspective – have told some serious truth. Or make some up. Consider how the theme of childhood 'innocence' has been developed in the novel as a whole.

CHAPTER NINE
SECTION 2 (pp. 213–23)

Focus on: themes and conclusions

— Every element in the description of Julie's cottage suggests home and comfort. This atmosphere is a fitting backdrop to her wish 'to draw him closer' and her delight to have 'her best hopes confirmed' (p. 215). Note the contrast between this situation and the situation between Stephen's parents when his mother broke the news of her pregnancy (pp. 171–7). This later moment seems a kind of repetition, but also an answer to, a healing of, all the pain that has come before.

EVALUATE WORDS AND PHRASES . . .
— Consider how the description of Julie's labour and the child's birth combines powerful imagery and homely realism, humorous detail and an impression of deep significance.

CONSIDER THE NARRATIVE SHAPE . . .
— Discuss how McEwan creates a sense of completeness to the conclusion of the novel.

CHAPTER NINE

Looking over Chapter Nine

QUESTIONS FOR ESSAYS OR DISCUSSION
1. 'He had a premonition followed instantly by a certainty . . . that all the sorrow, all the empty waiting had been enclosed within meaningful time, within the richest unfolding conceivable.' (p. 213). Discuss the significance of this thought of Stephen's to the theme of time in the novel as a whole.

2. How satisfactory do you find this chapter as a conclusion to *The Child in Time*?

Looking back over the whole novel

QUESTIONS FOR ESSAYS OR DISCUSSION
1. Discuss the validity of the claim that, 'For all its playfulness, *The Child in Time* is a moving and profound novel.'

2. 'There had to be a deeper patterning to time, its wrong

and right moments can't be that limited,' says Julie. How convincingly does *The Child in Time* prove its own thesis?

3. Is the ingenious architecture of *The Child in Time* too self-conscious to please?

4. 'McEwan has the surrealist knack of making the world gleam with a light that never was on land or sea.' Account for the descriptive power of McEwan's style.

Contexts, comparisons and complementary readings

THE CHILD IN TIME

These sections suggest contextual and comparative ways of reading three novels by McEwan. You can put your reading in a social, historical or literary context. You can make comparisons – again, social, literary or historical – with other texts or art works. Or you can choose complementary works (of whatever kind) – that is, art works, literary works, social reportage or facts that in some way illuminate the text by sidelights or interventions which you can make into a telling framework. Some of the suggested contexts are directly connected to the book, in that they give you precise literary or social frames in which to situate the novel. In turn, these are related either to the period within which the novel is set or to the time – now – when you are reading it. Some of these examples are designed to suggest books or other texts that may make useful sources for comparison (or for complementary purposes) when you are reading McEwan's work. Again, they may be related to literary or critical themes, or they may be relevant to social and cultural themes current 'then' or 'now'.

Focus on: the theme of time, science and art

RESEARCH . . .

— What was discovered about the nature of time in the last century and at the beginning of this one? Read Chapter One, 'Our Picture of the Universe', in *A Brief History of Time* (1988) by Stephen Hawking. As McEwan acknowledges in the interview, he is a writer who is much interested in the new theories of time that were being published by theorists and scientific thinkers in the last part of the twentieth century. *The Child in Time* was published in 1987. McEwan's was not the only novel to be influenced by the ideas that are found in Hawking's work. You might like to look at Jeanette Winterson's novel *Sexing the Cherry* (1989) for an example of another literary text that adapted current scientific theories for the purposes of a literary experiment. How does the content of either of these other texts – Hawking or Winterson – relate to, or compare with, the ideas about time explored in McEwan's *The Child in Time*?

COMPARE . . .

— Look at some well-known poems on the subject of time and loss. Examples (although there are many others) might include:

- Sonnet 60 by William Shakespeare
- 'To His Coy Mistress' by Andrew Marvell
- 'When I have fears' by John Keats
- 'Ozymandias' by Percy Bysshe Shelley
- 'Remember' by Christina Rossetti
- 'Felix Randal' by Gerard Manley Hopkins
- 'They all have lied that told me time would heal' by Edna St Vincent Millay
- 'Leaves' by Ted Hughes
- 'Becoming of Age' by Simon Armitage.

— What have any of these writers to say about time and its effects? How might their ideas connect with the ideas about time outlined or expressed in *The Child in Time*?

LIST AND ANALYSE VOCABULARY AND PHRASES . . .
— How do we describe time? What words or phrases do we use? Refer to a dictionary of quotations or of phrases to find expressions about time. What does our language say about the attitudes to time that have found their way into everyday life? Some expressions that you could consider might include: 'to make time for', 'to waste time', 'to have time', 'to lose time', 'to find the time', 'to be in time'. You will be able to think of others.
— What similar 'conventional' phrases about time can you pick out in *The Child in Time*? Where, and in what circumstances, are such phrases used pejoratively, sardonically or playfully?

Focus on: the theme of childhood

MAKE UP YOUR OWN STORY . . .
— Write a short story – no more than one page long – about some key event (large or small) that captures a child's view of the world. Tell it through the eyes of a child. Then – for five to ten minutes' worth of writing – try retelling the scene of Kate's abduction in *The Child in Time* (in Chapter 1) from the point of view of Kate. Or retell the story of Stephen's encounter with the little girl with the mole on her cheek (pp. 146–52) from her point of view. What difference does this change of narrative position make to your perception of the novel? This might relate to the significance of certain themes, the importance of a communicating language or a more broadly moral perspective . . . You decide on which you wish to focus.

71

COMPARE . . .

— Read the opening chapter of Charles Dickens's *Great Expectations* (1861). This life-changing event is presented from the child's point of view. Or is it?

Focus on: the theme of language

ANALYSE . . .

— Look out for characters in this novel who use language in order to manipulate other people's reactions. Look for those whose vocabulary or means of coherent expression is curtailed. Look also for those who set out to tell the truth as they really see it. And pay attention to the ways in which McEwan plays with language, showing how it can define life truthfully and how it can also deceive.

Focus on: the theme of men and women

READ . . .

— Study the following quotations about Margaret Thatcher, leader of the Conservative Party and the first woman Prime Minister in Britain from 1979 to 1990:

- 'The best man in Britain' – *Ronald Reagan*
- 'She's nice and cuddly' – *Paul Gascoigne*
- 'Trying to tell the Prime Minister anything is like making an important phone call and getting an answering machine' – *David Steele*
- 'The legs of Marilyn Monroe and the eyes of Genghis Khan' – *Alan Clark*

— *The Child in Time* was published in 1987 and for much of

the novel we are not explicitly told the gender of the Prime Minister in the story. The implication is that she is a woman, suggesting that some references to Mrs Thatcher may be there in the background. How do these sayings about her by real people who dealt with her relate to the portrayal of the character of 'the Prime Minister' in Ian McEwan's novel?

LIST AND ANALYSE VOCABULARY USED IN RELATION TO GENDER . . .

— Compile two lists: one for traits that you consider to be typical of men, and the other for traits that you think are typical of women. Where would you put such traits as: competitive, cooperative, conformist, creative, liking hierarchy and power, having a sense of justice, liking to organise others, submissive, liking machines, sincere, intuitive, emotionally aware, caring, altruistic, sensitive, respecting authority, emotional and open to change?

— Once you've made your lists, consider whether there are any hard facts that will support or refute these attributions: if there are, seek out some of those facts to test your thesis. Alternatively, use these lists as a starting point for a discussion (with yourself or others) about men's and women's attitudes to shared issues such as sex, family, parenting, hierarchy, friendship and work.

ANALYSE AND INTERPRET . . .

— Jokes can be wryly revealing of a culture's shared attitudes. What does each of these statements suggest about Western attitudes to relationships between men and women?:

- 'Men who don't understand women fall into two groups . . . bachelors and husbands' – *Jacques Languirand*
- 'If you never want to see a man again, say "I love you, I want to marry you, I want to have children." They leave skid marks' – *Rita Rudner*

- 'The longest sentence you can form with two words is, "I do"' – *H. L. Mencken*
- 'Running after women never hurt anybody; it's catching them that does the damage' – *Jack Davies*
- 'To be able to turn a man out into the garden and tell him to stay there until the next meal, is every woman's dream.' – *Virginia Graham*
- 'Women who can, do. Those who can't become feminists' – *Bobby Riggs*
- 'Why does a woman work for ten years to change a man's habits, and then complain that he's not the man she married?' – *Barbra Streisand*
- 'Love is ideal. Marriage is real. The confusion of the two shall never go unpunished' – *J. W. von Goethe*
- 'If you are married, it takes just one to make a quarrel' – *Ogden Nash*
- 'The only place men want depth in a woman is in her décolletage' – *Zsa Zsa Gabor*
- 'It's too bad that in marriage ceremonies they don't use the word "obey" any more. It used to lend a little humour to the occasion.' – *Lloyd Cory*

— Look for places in *The Child in Time* where characters make similar sweeping statements about men and women and their relationships. What purpose do those remarks serve: a) in creating the characterisation of the person who speaks them?; b) in relation to the working out of this theme through the whole novel?

— Read these two short newspaper articles:

'A sari saved four lives'
Nellore (AP). Dec. 2 (PTI) – A sari stood between four men and death during the cyclone that hit several parts of Andhra Pradesh recently.

The four men and a woman, belonging to Mambattu village of Nellore district, in a desperate bid to escape the fury of the cyclone and the resulting deluge on November 14 tied the sari of the woman to a tree and clung to it precariously.

The men were saved, but unfortunately the woman who lent her sari for the survival attempt died because of exposure to the cold and rain.

The Pioneer, Lucknow, 1985

'Sex boycott turns on taps'
A month after women in the southern Turkish village of Sirt began refusing to have sex until their men provided them with running water, the government has agreed to supply enough pipes to build a system.

The husbands will now lay the pipes from a water source five miles away. The Anatolia news agency did not say whether the bedroom boycott would remain until the system was completed.

Daily Telegraph, Thursday 16 August 2001

— What do these stories tell us, implicitly or explicitly, about underlying assumptions concerning gender characterisation and hierarchy? Think particularly about the value content of the language used in each article. Is either of these stories funny? Or are they both tragic?
— Then look through *The Child in Time* and pick out examples of places where the narrative method mimics this 'newspaper' style of writing about men and women. What critical purpose do these passages serve, and how do they make the reader re-examine conventions and assumptions on this theme?

Focus on: the theme of public policy and individual liberty

SEARCH . . .

— *The Child in Time* was published in 1987. Find out about the
1980s. Which party was in power in Britain? What was the political climate like? The novel is set at an unspecified time, by implication shortly after 1987. As you read it, ask yourself which aspects
of the society it depicts represent trends already in place in the
1980s. Does the novel still speak about contemporary political
positions on issues such as public services and childcare?

— On which areas of private behaviour does your national
government legislate? (Examples might be alcohol use, sexual
behaviour and the use of corporal punishment by parents.) Do
an information search using government websites (such as the
UK website www.open.gov.uk). Do you think that government
interference is legitimate in these sorts of private activities?
When might such interference be inappropriate?

Focus on: the theme of child abduction and its effects

COMMENT ON . . .

— In *The Child in Time* we never find out what happened to
Kate, but it is every parent's worst nightmare that the lost child
might have died in tragic circumstances. Why do you imagine
that none of the characters in the novel ever mentions, or even
seems to think of, this possibility? In what ways might this
have been a different novel if these fears and possible anxieties had been faced head-on?

COMPARE . . .

— Read Ruth Rendell's novel *A Fatal Inversion* (1991), which
includes a story about a child who is abducted and an account
of the results, both for the abductor and for the bereaved

family. Compare the portrayal of that event with the similar story in *The Child in Time*. In what ways do these two novels draw very different moral conclusions?

Focus on: the theme of absence and presence

CONSIDER ...
— In 1922 the famous painting by Leonardo da Vinci called 'La Gioconda' – 'the smiling woman' – but most well known as the 'Mona Lisa' was stolen from the Louvre Museum in Paris. (It was later returned, and can still be seen there.) While the picture was lost, the museum authorities decided simply to leave the space on the wall unfilled and went on illuminating it, as if the picture were still there. During the years of its absence, many hundreds of thousands of people went to look at the empty space – more than had been to look at the picture in previous years when it had actually been there. Why?
— Can you visualise what the 'Mona Lisa' looks like in your mind's eye? Have you ever been to the Louvre to see it? If not, how do you know what picture we are talking about? Why do you still feel as though you 'know' the picture. Consider the implications of the cultural – or commercialised – knowledge that we share.

VINTAGE
LIVING
TEXTS

Enduring Love

IN CLOSE-UP

Reading guides for

ENDURING LOVE

THE TITLE . . .

— McEwan's titles always have a depth to them. There is a pun in *Enduring Love*. Is 'enduring' an adjective describing the quality of love? Or is it a verb, a present participle describing how to cope with love? What difference does it make?

— Examine this question again after you have read to the end of the novel. Ask yourself if your attitude to the title has changed, and how you think it relates to what happens in the book as a whole.

BEFORE YOU BEGIN TO READ . . .

If you look at the interview with McEwan, you will see that he discusses the themes of:

- Science
- Delusion
- The Romantic tradition
- Relationships.

81

Other themes that are relevant to *Enduring Love* include:

- The 'conflict' between science and religion
- The value of myths and stories in uncovering truth
- Love
- Obsession
- Stalker and victim
- Trust
- The disruption of normal, everyday patterns by a strange event
- Storytelling and point of view
- Art versus science.

Reading activities: detailed analysis

CHAPTER ONE
SECTION I (pp. 1–3)

Focus on: openings

ANALYSE . . .

— Many readers remember the opening of *Enduring Love* because of the way it creates a sense of gripping suspense. The chief effect of this first section is to suggest that something terrible is about to happen. How is this achieved? Note in particular all the references to a moment of transformation – from what to what is merely implied. Focus on the paragraph 'I'm holding back . . .' Which words and images here imply a reassuring order that is about to be unsettled?

— Reread the first section (from 'The beginning is simple to mark . . .' to '. . . of help.'). What does this opening tell you about the narrator's state of mind?

— This novel is partly about telling stories. A major theme will be how people tell stories to make sense of experience. What in this first section draws our attention to the fact that this is a narrative account – life turned into a story?

Focus on: narrative point of view

ANALYSE THE NARRATIVE CONSTRUCTION . . .

— How does McEwan employ the narrative viewpoint in this section, and to what effect? The narrator is a character involved in the events. How is irony used to create tension? Consider the effect of those phrases that imply that the narrator's life will be irrevocably changed by what is about to take place (e.g. 'Knowing what I know now', 'innocent of the grief this entanglement would bring').

— Why does he give the buzzard's imagined perspective?

— Read each of the paragraphs in the first section in turn. Then ask some of the following questions: where is the narrator positioning himself? Is he telling this story in the moment? Or is he looking back on events? Is he inside his own body, looking at what is happening through his own eyes? Or is he imagining himself outside his subjective experience?

Focus on: methods of storytelling

EXAMINE . . .

— Consider the opening sentence of each of the paragraphs in this first section: 'The beginning is simple to mark'; 'I see us from three hundred feet up'; 'What was Clarissa doing?'; 'I'm holding back, delaying the information'; 'What were we running towards?'; 'We were running towards a catastrophe . . .' What kind of a story do these disjointed sentences tell?

— Recall the ways in which film uses different narrative techniques. What happens if something is filmed in close-up? Or long-distance? What difference does it make to the telling of a story if a director chooses to use a split screen? Find places in this section where a 'filmic' narrative technique is adopted.

Focus on: themes

DISTINGUISH . . .
— The ideas of clear sight and delusion will become important themes: how are they established in the opening section? Pay attention whenever the word 'clarity' (p. 3) is used later in the novel.

CHAPTER ONE
SECTION 2 (pp. 3–7)

Focus on: characterisation

SEARCH . . .
— Many authors name their characters to reflect something special about them. So why is Clarissa in *Enduring Love* called Clarissa? It is the name of a famous early epistolary novel (a novel made up of letters) by Samuel Richardson, which was published in eight volumes (1747–9).
— Look up a synopsis of *Clarissa* in a literary dictionary – the *Oxford Companion to English Literature* would be a good choice – or read the novel (or part of it anyway), then think about the reasons why McEwan might have decided to call this character Clarissa. You could also look up Virginia Woolf's novel *Mrs Dalloway* (1925), where the main character's first name is Clarissa.
— While you were reading the first chapter we asked you to pay attention to the word 'clarity'. Look up the word in a dictionary. How might this word relate to Clarissa's name? What could the assonance – the similarity of sound – suggest about Clarissa's role in the novel as a whole?
— Ian McEwan talks about this in the interview. If he

wanted Clarissa to be 'wrong', then how ironic is his choice of name?

Focus on: normality versus catastrophe

CONSIDER . . .
— This section portrays events prior to the opening crisis in reassuringly familiar terms. How does McEwan convey a sense of normality? Consider how, during the episode at Heathrow, the narrator views the unknown characters around him in ways that make them familiar, both to him and to us.

EXAMINE THE VOCABULARY . . .
— McEwan often uses aesthetic correspondences to create a sense of inner coherence in his fiction. Look for images in this section that parallel details from pp. 1–3, but in a more reassuring form.

Focus on: truth as fictional narrative

OUTLINE AND INTERPRET . . .
— Begin to explore the ways in which characters in this novel interpret the world through narratives. The narrator observes the people at Heathrow as if they are playing out a drama. Clarissa is attempting to reach the truth about Keats's private dramas through the stories he told in his letters. As the novel progresses, note every time you spot an occasion when characters try to understand the world by telling stories about it. This is seen to be equally true of the arts (Clarissa is a university teacher of English literature), of the sciences (the narrator is a science journalist) and of the deluded systems of an obsessive mind (see Chapter Eleven).

CHAPTER ONE
SECTION 3 (pp. 7–16)

Focus on: contrast, control, measuring moral responsibility

LIST THE WORD CHOICE . . .
— 'let me freeze the frame – there's a security in stillness' (p. 12). Telling the story in retrospect allows the narrator a control over events that he did not have at the time. He exercises that control to analyse exactly what happened, and to consider who was to blame. Read from p. 12 to the end of Chapter One and consider the way in which the narrator analyses a moment of tragedy. Pick out the phrases that show that he does so with a scientist's eye for objective exactness.

INTERPRET . . .
— Looking back on Chapter One, consider how much we know about the narrator so far. We have not yet been told his name or his occupation. What things do we actually know about him? Consider why McEwan has told us certain bits of information by this point, but not others.

CHAPTER ONE

Looking over Chapter One

QUESTIONS FOR DISCUSSION OR ESSAYS
1. Analyse the way that narrative, and ideas about narrative, are developed in this first chapter.

2. Consider the theme of catastrophe and its effects.

3. 'Even without the balloon the day would have been

marked for memory' (p. 3). Discuss the role and function of memory.

4. Consider the significance of individual social responsibility as it is set out in relation to the events that take place in Chapter One.

CHAPTER TWO
(pp. 17–27)

Focus on: themes

DISTINGUISH AND LIST . . .

— Read the first three paragraphs of Chapter Two. It is typical of McEwan's writing that many of the themes that have previously emerged are now re-emphasised explicitly – a technique that lends aesthetic cohesion to his narrative. Underline phrases that express the key themes of the novel so far.

CONSIDER . . .

— The word 'tragedy' is used twice in this chapter to denote Logan's death, by the narrator on p. 18 and by Parry on p. 25. Consider how they use the same word differently. Consider the context in which this word is used, and how this affects its meaning. Look up the strict meaning of 'tragedy' in the glossary of literary terms.

— Does 'mere tragedy' mean 'only' or 'pure' tragedy? How do conventional literary definitions of tragedy relate to what happens in the opening scenes of the novel? How is the theme of tragedy handled in the novel as a whole?

ANALYSE AND CRITICALLY EVALUATE . . .

— Read the description of the narrator's recurring nightmare on p. 18. Consider the idea that dreams are another form of narrative, which the mind employs to make sense of experience; but, in contrast to the narrator's reflective, measured analysis of events, dreams operate on the level of symbol and the dramatisation of emotional impulses ('I did not think about the dream then so much as experience its emotional wash' [p. 18]). In the interview McEwan describes how the initial idea for his novel *The Child in Time* came partly out of a dream. You might like to look at that extract in the light of these 'dream' images in *Enduring Love*.

— Look at the narrator's description of seeing Logan's corpse on pp. 22–3 ('The sheep that had hardly ... shelter of the trees'). How does he react? He is clearly intellectually interested; does he experience any emotions? Consider the word 'inanimate' (p. 23) and its etymology. What does it mean? In what sense is he using it here: absence of life, or absence of soul? What's the difference? What is meant by 'soul'? What seems to be the narrator's attitude towards the idea of a human soul?

— Logan is, in one sense, the second dead man to figure in the novel: the first is Keats. In what sense, for Clarissa, is Keats not wholly dead?

ANALYSE WORDS AND MEANING . . .

— Read the conversation between Parry and the narrator. Think carefully about the impulses that guide the narrator's reactions here, especially the references that he makes to the conventions of social engagement.

— Now analyse Parry's words and actions. In what ways does Parry manipulate the narrator?

— Look at the end of the chapter, 'Jed Parry's love and pity' (p. 27). This is the second mention in the novel of the word 'love'. Earlier Clarissa had said of Keats and Fanny Brawne that 'he loved her so much' – a love that endured to his death despite its impossibility, and that endures after his death in his letters. Parry's 'love' will endure, driving the plot of the novel; and the narrator must (in another sense) endure it. Consider the title again: could *Enduring Love* mean both 'love that endures' and 'suffering unwanted love'?

— Note every occurrence of the word 'love' as the novel progresses and consider what it means in each instance.

CHAPTER TWO

Looking over Chapter Two

QUESTIONS FOR DISCUSSION OR ESSAYS

1. Consider the development of character in this chapter.

2. Analyse the revivalist language of Jed Parry and contrast it with Joe's humanist terms.

CHAPTER THREE
(pp. 28–37)

Focus on: making sense of a traumatic experience by turning it into a story

ANALYSE WORDS AND PHRASES . . .

In the last chapter Jed Parry tried to persuade Joe to pray by arguing that 'God has brought us together in this tragedy and we have to, you know, make whatever sense of it we can' (p. 25). Later on he says, 'It's a gift.' He is speaking of the accident that has brought them together, but he is still imputing an agency – that of God's design – to an incident that is (many

people would think) merely coincidental. Jed's seeking an explanation and shape for events in the plan of an all-seeing God
is one way of telling a story about experience.

— Read through Chapter Three and see how many times the
idea of telling a story to 'explain' events is posited.

— Where do we hear Jed's phrase about 'making sense' again?
What effect does this repetition have on you?

— 'The unaltered array of my breakfast coffee cup and newspaper seemed blasphemous' (p. 28). What does Joe mean? What
images does the choice of vocabulary here convey? What does
this 'array' blaspheme? What does it matter that the display of
objects is 'unaltered'?

— Write down any words or terms used in this chapter that are
descriptions of versions of practical storytelling. Begin by looking at p. 28 at the list: 'a post-mortem, a re-living, a de-briefing,
the rehearsal of grief, and the exorcism of terror'.

DEFINE AND DISTINGUISH . . .
— At the end of the first paragraph the narrator says, 'We
sat facing each other and began' (p. 28). What do they begin?
Why?

— How many stories get told in the chapter?

— What does Joe mean when he says that he and Clarissa
told the events of the day to their friends in 'the married style'
(p. 36)?

— What is the effect of what happens at the end of the chapter (p. 37)?

CHAPTER THREE

Looking over Chapter Three

QUESTION FOR DISCUSSION OR ESSAYS
1.   In relation to *Enduring Love* discuss: a) the extraordinary in the everyday, b) the everyday in the extraordinary.

CHAPTER FOUR
(pp. 38–45)

Focus on: notions of order and control

DISCUSS . . .
— In this chapter Joe is trying to re-establish some order and pattern in his life after the catastrophe of the day before. What is the first thing he cites as something that might give back that reassurance?
— Think about how we create the shapes in our lives: what written objects help to make that order? How far can engagement diaries, address books, timetables, daily journals (for instance) be said to represent the reality or the whole truth of anyone's life? Consider how this question is worked out in the novel as a whole.

LIST AND SEARCH . . .
— Count up how many stories about science or references to the stories of historical events are told to us in these few pages.
— If you know about any of these events or theories, think about how they may reflect on what is happening in the novel at this point.
— If you don't, then choose one that interests you, find out

more about it from reference books and then think about its relevance to this moment in the novel.

CRITICALLY EVALUATE THE VOCABULARY . . .

— While all these stories are being offered to us, Joe admits to being distracted. Work out where he first tells us about this, and then underline or write down the words he uses each time he refers to it again.

— What effect does this counterpointed theme of disorder, or lack of control, have on you as the reader?

— How does the imagery related to 'contamination' build up? How does this metaphoric strand create a separate, linguistic order?

CONSIDER . . .

— Why does Joe put the kicked-over marigolds back into their jar on p. 44? How does this connect to the theme of control?

— Tell yourself or your group the story of how you did, or might have done, something similarly superstitious in the hope of a positive outcome, which was actually entirely unrelated to the action. Why did you do whatever it was? What did you hope to achieve? What actually happened? How can you connect your own experience with Joe's in this chapter, and elsewhere in the novel as a whole?

CHAPTER FIVE
(pp. 46–53)

Focus on: narrative and unreliability

ANALYSE AND JUSTIFY . . .

In this chapter the narrator draws attention to himself as a narrator. Joe is a writer on popular science and at the centre here is the story of how he composes an article for a magazine. Once it is done, however, he finds that he does not trust his own argument.

— Look carefully through the chapter and note each time the question of truth or untruth arises, and how one discriminates between them.

— The chapter begins with a reference to Joe's last meeting of the day. 'I had a second meeting that day – I was on a jury judging a science book prize ...' (p. 46). Why are the words 'jury' and 'judging' significant?

— In what ways do we decide whether or not something is 'true'? Or why one thing is 'better' than another? You might think about this in relation to a court case where the men and women of the jury have to decide the guilt or innocence of the accused. On what do they base their decision?

— Or you might think about this in relation to adjudicating a prize. How do you decide on the merits or demerits of one thing over another?

COMPARE AND PLACE IN CONTEXT ...

— The story that Joe tells in the imaginary article he is writing is about how the narrative method of nineteenth-century science influenced (and was influenced by) the narrative method of the novel. A similar argument was proposed by Gillian Beer in *Darwin's Plots*. Read this book – or part of it. Consider how ideas about storytelling function in the novel as a whole.

— Joe begins Chapter Five by telling us that he 'needed to talk' to Clarissa (p. 46). By the end of the chapter he still has not told her about Jed Parry and the phone call (pp. 52–3). What is more, he has unplugged the phone. How does this make you feel about how far you can trust Joe as a narrator?

Looking over Chapters Four and Five

QUESTIONS FOR DISCUSSION OR ESSAYS

1. 'A first-person narrator is always an unreliable narrator.' Discuss in relation to the narrative technique and characterisation in *Enduring Love*.

2. Consider the functions of storytelling in making order out of chaos, as set out in *Enduring Love*.

CHAPTER SIX
(pp. 54–60)

Focus on: figurative language

CRITICALLY EVALUATE WORD CHOICE . . .

— Read this chapter through, then underline all the different kinds of figurative language you can find. This will include metaphors (where one thing is compared to another to which it is not related) similes (where something is said to be 'like' something else) and synecdoche (where a part of a thing stands in for the whole and vice versa). If you are uncertain about any literary terms, look up 'figurative language' in a Glossary of Literary Terms.

— Now look at the passage that deals with Joe's rerun of the events of the balloon disaster. He is highly aware of his own use of language here.

— Joe is a writer, language is his medium. Ian McEwan is a writer, language is his medium. Why do you think that this particular passage pays so much attention to words and their literary uses?

CHAPTER SIX

Looking over Chapter Six

QUESTIONS FOR DISCUSSION OR ESSAYS

1. Consider how many times we have now heard the story of the ballooning accident and discuss how each of those versions relates to the others.

2. *'Enduring Love* is a novel telling the story of telling the story.' Discuss.

CHAPTER SEVEN
(pp. 61–8)

Focus on: clichés in speech and scene

LINGUISTIC RESPONSE . . .

— Read the paragraph on p. 67 that begins, 'He said more along these lines . . .' and ends, '. . . even though our household was no more than this turd-strewn pavement'. The narrator here thinks about how the words he and Jed are saying to each other are dictated not by real feeling (at least not on Joe's part), but by certain conventions of speech that belong to 'domestic drama'.

— Underline all the phrases in their conversation that sound like lines from a soap opera or a film.

— Why are such phrases so familiar? What situations do they suggest? Are they ever appropriate in lived life? Have you ever used such lines? If so, why?

Focus on: the theme of love

SEARCH AND COMPARE . . .

— This is the second time that Joe and Jed have met. Compare their first meeting on pp. 23–7. What is different about this time? What is the same?

— How many different kinds of love are cited or referred to in this chapter?

DISCUSS . . .

— Who is in love with whom here? Consider some of Joe's phrases: 'He was just about young enough to be my son' (pp. 61–2); 'I thought perhaps I was being parodied' (p. 63); 'He looked away and said nothing which I took as confirmation' (p. 64); 'I was feeling suffocated' (p. 64); 'I should have walked on, but his intensity held me for the moment and I had just sufficient curiosity to echo him' (p. 65); 'As we pulled away I looked back. He was standing in the road, waving to me forlornly but looking, without question, like a man blessed in love' (p. 68).

CHAPTER EIGHT
(pp. 69–78)

Focus on: the value of myths and stories in uncovering truth

LIST AND ANALYSE . . .

— On p. 73 Joe says, 'This moment, as well as the one in the field when Clarissa handed me a bottle of wine, might serve as starting point . . .' Note down every time Joe thinks about how and why he is telling a story.

— What do you make of the story of Joe's own career here (pp. 75–7)?

PERFORM . . .

— Write a mini-play where the dialogue consists entirely of a set of messages on an answerphone. Look again at the story of Jed's messages in the light of your attempt.

CHAPTER EIGHT

Looking over Chapter Eight

QUESTION FOR DISCUSSION OR ESSAYS

1. Consider the use of first-person narratives in the story so far.

CHAPTER NINE
(pp. 79–88)

Focus on: point of view

COMPARE AND ANALYSE THE LANGUAGE . . .

— Read Chapter Twenty-Nine of George Eliot's *Middlemarch* (1871–2), which begins, 'One morning, some weeks after her arrival at Lowick, Dorothea – but why always Dorothea?'

— How does this narrative digression on Eliot's part compare with that given here by McEwan as Joe takes up Clarissa's point of view?

— Think about the use of personal pronouns in the third person, 'he' and 'she' instead of 'I'. Where is the narrating 'I' that we have become used to?

— And what about the verb tenses used here? Are they more often past tense? Or present?

CREATE . . .

— Write out a scene where you have had a blazing row with someone important to you. But write it from the point of view of the other person, and then look again at Joe's account of Clarissa's attitudes and reactions.

Focus on: language and style

SEARCH . . .

— Read pp. 86–8 carefully, from 'But now they seem cast in a play they cannot stop . . .' to '. . . "Well, fuck off then," Joe shouts to her departing back.'

— Look at a passage of dialogue from any play or soap opera where the characters are having an argument, and compare the set speech patterns of the dialogue there with what happens here. A play by Harold Pinter might be a good place to look: Act II of *The Birthday Party* (1958), for instance; or the end of Henrik Ibsen's *Hedda Gabler* (1890); or the end of Act I of Samuel Beckett's *Waiting for Godot* (1955). Obviously each one of these plays is presenting a very stylised dialogue. How does that compare with the language of a scene from a television soap opera? And how do either or both compare with Joe's sense of the stereotyped language that he and Jed are using to one another?

CHAPTER TEN
(pp. 89–92)

Focus on: symbols

TRACE AND ANALYSE . . .

— Write down all the things that feature in this chapter either as something 'real' (like Joe's right shoe with the hole in it) or

99

as something imagined (like the umbrella he doesn't go back for).

— Now make a list of what those things might signify, what they might mean to you or anyone else, what they might symbolise in different cultures.

— Consider how particular objects in our culture acquire meanings far beyond their original functional uses. Shoes, for instance, are a good place to start. What does it mean to have a hole in a shoe, both literally and metaphorically? What does it mean if you are wearing running shoes, as opposed to high-heeled stilettos? What might a picture of either on its own 'mean'? What does the ancient Chinese practice of foot-binding suggest to you? (If you don't know about this, find out.) What does *The Red Shoes* mean to you? Either read the story by Hans Christian Andersen or see the film by Michael Powell (1948). Use your findings to analyse Joe's state of mind at this point in the novel.

CONSIDER YOUR OWN RESPONSE . . .
— What are curtains for? To shut out the world? To shut in? Which? What else? What are they made of? Where do you see them? What different kinds are there? What do they do in different situations?

CHAPTER ELEVEN
(pp. 93–8)

Focus on: storytelling method and point of view

SEARCH . . .
This is the first time that an actual letter appears in this book, but it won't be the last. Novels written in the eighteenth century

were often 'epistolary' in form – that is, written as if they were a series of letters.

— Find a novel that is written in letters. You might begin by looking up 'epistolary novel' in the *Oxford Companion to English Literature*. Otherwise you could try a twentieth-century novel, such as *84 Charing Cross Road* (1971) by Helene Hanff or *Daddy-Long-Legs* (1912) by Jean Webster. Or find out about novels that are written in the form of a diary. You could try *The Secret Diary of Adrian Mole aged 13¾* (1982) by Sue Townsend, for instance. What difference does it make to your attitudes to the events and characters in a novel if they are presented as letters or a diary?

CHAPTER ELEVEN

Looking over Chapter Eleven

QUESTION FOR DISCUSSION OR ESSAYS

1. 'Our deeds determine us, as much as we determine our deeds' – George Eliot. Discuss, in relation to *Enduring Love*.

CHAPTER TWELVE

(pp. 99–107)

Focus on: the theme of trust

EXAMINE YOUR OWN REACTIONS . . .

— Consider Joe's analysis of how the trust between him and Clarissa has broken down. Jot down each of the things that make the situation worse.

— How do you feel about your own relation as a reader to

Joe as narrator? Do you trust him? Why do you suppose McEwan adds that remark of Clarissa's on p. 100, '... "His writing's rather like yours."'?

CHAPTER TWELVE

Looking over Chapter Twelve

QUESTIONS FOR DISCUSSION OR ESSAYS

1. Consider how Ian McEwan uses literary allusion and/or contemporary news stories as structuring devices.

2. 'Love makes this little room an everywhere' – John Donne. How might this idea relate to the truths and the deceptions of love in McEwan's *Enduring Love*?

CHAPTER THIRTEEN
(pp. 108–17)

Focus on: the theme of trust

ANALYSE AND COMPARE ...

— Although John Logan is now dead, his wife has lost all trust in who he was, who she thought he was and how she trusted him. Look back at the process of the breakdown of trust that you analysed between Joe and Clarissa in the last chapter, and think about how the same process is happening between Jean Logan and her reconstructed memory of her relations with her husband.

— What do you think is Jean Logan's attitude to Joe? Or to the police who investigated the circumstances of the accident? Whom does she trust?

Focus on: place

CONSIDER VOCABULARY AND WORD CHOICE ...
We move here for the first time to a third, domestic scene.
The previous ones are Joe and Clarissa's flat and Jed Parry's
house, as described by him in Chapter Eleven.
— How does McEwan (or Joe as narrator) set up Mrs
Logan's house? Underline specific words and phrases that
describe the special feeling in and of the house, as well as
practical facts about the house, the rooms, the garden and
the furniture.
— How does this scene compare with the descriptions of the
other two domestic scenes so far?

Focus on: speech patterns

DEFINE AND EVALUATE EXPRESSIONS ...
— What kind of language is Mrs Logan talking? Focus on
her vocabulary where you find words like 'condolences, con-
solations, that kind of thing' (p. 110); 'I'm the mad one, of
course' (p. 111); 'There, there, Mrs Logan! Don't go fretting
about things that don't concern you ...' (p. 111); 'Did you look
for fingerprints?' (p. 115); 'If she comes near this house ... I'll
kill her. God help me, but I will' (p. 117).
— Where else might you find phrases like these? Why are they
so familiar?

CHAPTER FOURTEEN
(pp. 118–25)

Focus on: the theme of childhood

COMPARE AND CONTRAST . . .

The Logan children are the only children we actually get to meet in *Enduring Love*. But children and childhood are major themes in many of McEwan's books.

— Read the first chapter of McEwan's *The Child in Time* and consider the ways in which you might make connections between the ideas of childhood that are presented in each of the two novels.

— On p. 123 of *Enduring Love* Leo says, 'But this is our palace and I'm the king and she's the queen and I only come out when she gives the signal.' So at this point a game between the two children takes us back to the curtain question and the 'meanings' attached to things that we were looking at in Chapter Eight (p. 78), and which occurs again in Chapter Ten (p. 92). Joe now has the answer (pp. 123–4). Work through each of these three 'curtain' passages and write down the word sequence that ends up providing the key to the explanation of Jed's behaviour that means so much to Joe.

— These children will appear again later in the novel. Look out for that appearance and remember to compare the two scenes.

— Once you have found the place where the children appear again and have read that later section, you might consider why it is that McEwan has given Leo and Rachael – and not anyone else – the passage of dialogue that gives Joe the clue to the curtain problem.

Focus on: *the theme of obsession*

SEARCH . . .
— Look in newspapers for accounts of obsessives who 'stalk' celebrities or people whom they know. What examples can you find of maniacally patterned behaviour along the lines of de Clérambault's syndrome?

Focus on: *narrative structure*

COMMENT ON THE PLOT DEVELOPMENT . . .
— Look at p. 122 where Joe says, 'At last, we were at the centre of the story. I was about to be accused, and I had to interrupt her. I wanted my own account in first . . .'
— What does Joe mean? What is going on here? What is he worried about?

CHAPTER FOURTEEN

Looking over Chapter Fourteen

QUESTIONS FOR DISCUSSION OR ESSAYS
1. Consider how this chapter has developed any of the following themes:

● The significance of childhood experience
● The ways in which events shape a character's attitudes
● The language of traumatic experience (or the failure of expression in the face of trauma).

2. 'Was my life to be entirely subordinate to other people's obsessions?' (p. 121). Consider how the theme of obsession is being played out by at least three characters portrayed in the novel.

CHAPTER FIFTEEN
(pp. 126–32)

Focus on: returning to beginnings

COMPARE AND ANALYSE . . .
— In the beginning section of this chapter Joe returns to the scene of the ballooning accident. Compare and contrast the scene as it is described in Chapter One with the way it is described here.
— What has changed in Joe's two analyses of the events of that day?

Focus on: the theme of love

DISCUSS . . .
— *Enduring Love* is a novel of 245 pages; p. 128 is just about halfway through. Read the passage on p. 128 from 'I began to return across the field towards my car . . .' to '. . . what could I learn about Parry that would restore me to Clarissa?'
— Think about how the theme of love has developed so far. What kinds of lovers have we met? What kinds of love?
— Explore the notion set out here that the obsessive syndrome attributed to Parry by Joe 'was a dark, distorting mirror that reflected and parodied a brighter world of lovers whose reckless abandon to their cause was sane'.

CHAPTER FIFTEEN

Looking over Chapter Fifteen

QUESTIONS FOR DISCUSSION OR ESSAYS
1. Discuss the theme of innocence versus experience.

2. Consider either the function of 'parody' or the function of 'reflection' as played out in the novel.

CHAPTER SIXTEEN
(pp. 133–8)

Focus on: point of view

COMPARE . . .

— Look back at Chapter Eleven (pp. 93–8) where we last saw a letter from Jed to Joe. Compare the two chapters. In what ways is the presentation of Jed's point of view still the same? In what ways has it changed?

SEARCH . . .

On p. 134 Jed Parry refers to a couple of the subjects that Joe has written about, specifically the carbon-dating of the Turin shroud and the theory that part of the Old Testament in the Bible was written by a woman. On this last, you might like to look at a book edited by Harold Bloom and David Rosenberg called *The Book of J* (1990).

— Find out about one of these subjects and consider how it might relate to the themes of the novel.

EVALUATE WORD CHOICE . . .

— Write up a list of all the words in Jed's letter that relate to the language of faith. Then look at a Bible, the Book of Common Prayer, the Koran or the Jewish Cabbala and see how many similar words you can extract and how many are used in different senses. How does the narrative manipulate the reader in relation to your attitude to Jed?

CHAPTER SIXTEEN

Looking over Chapter Sixteen

QUESTION FOR DISCUSSION OR ESSAY

1. Earlier on Joe said to himself about Parry, 'I am in a relationship.' How is that 'relationship' worked out or extended in this chapter?

CHAPTER SEVENTEEN
(pp. 139–49)

Focus on: narrative structure

TRACE AND INTERPRET . . .

— Read through this chapter carefully. It starts 'I don't know what led to it, but we were lying face to face in bed . . .' – and ends with that same scene as Clarissa announces that she's going to sleep in another room. But in between there are at least two (and possibly three) narrative digressions away from that 'real' scene.

— Work out exactly which passages relate to which part of the narrative. Consider how each passage relates to the others. What shape is the narrative creating here? What does that patterning suggest to you about Joe's state of mind? What effect does it have on your attitude to Joe?

— Look at p. 143 where Joe says, 'On one occasion, watched by Parry, I lingered by the privet and ran my hands along it to imprint it with a message, and then I turned his way and looked at him.' Now think about what this action might suggest. Where have you seen this before? What might this narrative event be pointing towards? How are you, the reader, meant to respond to this?

— What other structuring devices of events, references or

allusions can you find in this chapter that are designed to guide you towards some judgement on Joe's state of mind?

Focus on: the themes of love and relationships

IMAGINE . . .
— Think about all the things Clarissa says to Joe on pp. 148–9. How would you try to talk to someone you love but believe to be deluded about some serious matter? How effective are Clarissa's attempts to get through to Joe?

CHAPTER EIGHTEEN
(pp. 150–61)

Focus on: the theme of obsession

SEARCH AND COMPARE . . .
— Look in any newspaper and see how often the word 'obsession' is used. Or just make a mental note every time you hear the word in everyday conversations or on the radio or television. In your opinion, does it always apply to the case in hand? Is the word ever used – again, in your opinion – incorrectly?

Focus on: narrative form

EXAMINE YOUR OWN REACTION AND PERFORM . . .
— On pp. 158–61 Joe tells a number of stories about being in 'two places at once'. This notion is a common experience. Try to recall some time in your life when this seemed vividly to happen to you. Then tell that story to somebody else.
— Think about how you structure your telling when, by definition, you have to convey two scenes simultaneously.
— Consider what happens to you when you are reading a

novel. In what ways are you, as reader, even in that ordinary situation, actually being 'in two places at once'? How do all of these shaping narrative patterns compare with the techniques and issues discussed in the novel as a whole?

RETELL . . .

— Using the account Joe gives us of how he lodged his complaint at the police station, on pp. 154–8, put yourself in the position of Linley the detective, and imagine how he would tell Joe's story to his wife that evening.

CHAPTER EIGHTEEN

Looking over Chapter Eighteen

QUESTIONS FOR DISCUSSION OR ESSAYS

1. 'Love can only be explained once it is lost.' Discuss.

2. Consider this proposition in relation to *Enduring Love*. 'The public story always perverts the truth of the private story.'

CHAPTER NINETEEN
(pp. 162–73)

Focus on: methods of storytelling

COMPARE . . .

— This chapter presents the second catastrophe to take place in the novel. Compare the way this event is presented with the way in which the ballooning accident is presented in the first chapter. What is the same? What is different?

— Consider your own reactions. How familiar are you by

now with Joe's (or McEwan's through Joe's) narrative techniques?

SEARCH . . .
— Clarissa's godfather Jocelyn tells a story here about the discovery of DNA. Find out what you can about this story and about the characters involved.
— When Joe gives Clarissa his present he says, 'Beauty is truth, truth beauty'. Where does the quotation come from? When you have found it, look carefully at the lines. Look at different editions and take note of how the punctuation of these lines varies. What difference does the placing of the inverted commas make to the meaning? How might this statement or equation relate to the themes of the novel as a whole?

COMPARE . . .
— Clarissa tells a story, on pp. 167–170, about Keats and Wordsworth. Find out as much as you can about this event. You might read Robert Gittings's biography *John Keats* (1962), which is mentioned on p. 169. How does this story relate to the events of the novel?

LIST AND COMMENT ON . . .
Look back at Chapter Eighteen where Joe was talking about 'being in two places at once'. How does the narrative in this chapter display the same patterning of doubleness?

CHAPTER TWENTY
SECTION 1 (pp. 174–82)

Focus on: point of view

SUMMARISE . . .

— Clarissa tells Joe not to 'go on about your usual stuff' (p. 175), and then he does just that, immediately launching into an explanation of how Jed Parry is to blame for the shooting. What does the policeman make of this? What do you make of it?

— On p. 179 the policeman says that 'educated people . . . book writers and all that' must keep journals and records and know what really happened. How does this relate: a) to the question about what flavour ice cream they were eating? and b) to the themes of the novel as a whole?

CHAPTER TWENTY
SECTION 2 (pp. 182–8)

Focus on: the theme of obsession

CONSIDER THE LANGUAGE . . .

— 'He wasn't in his usual place' (p. 182). What more do these words mean than they appear to mean? What does this suggest about Joe's interior emotional map?

— Look at the words at the end of the chapter on p. 188. Where might you have heard them before? How appropriate are they in Joe's situation?

Focus on: the theme of storytelling

CONSIDER

— Joe's decision to try to contact Johnny looks like a simple plot device. But how does that decision connect to the themes of the novel as a whole?

CHAPTER TWENTY

Looking over Chapter Twenty

QUESTION FOR DISCUSSION OR ESSAYS
1. 'Past and future are both the same in that neither are real, both are imagined.' Discuss, in relation to *Enduring Love*.

CHAPTER TWENTY-ONE
(pp. 189–203)

Focus on: narrative structure

COMPARE AND CONTRAST . . .
— This is the third car journey that Joe has made out of town: the first was to the Chilterns in Chapter One, the second was to Oxford to see Mrs Logan. What mood is evoked in each? How has Joe changed through the first, second and third journey?
— This is also the third (or fourth, if you count Jed's description of his house) occasion when we are shown a domestic space. How does this house compare with Clarissa and Joe's flat and with the Logans' house in North Oxford? Think about both constituent physical elements and atmosphere.

LIST THE VOCABULARY . . .
— Write down as many words and phrases as you can that are to do with Joe's precarious state of mind. How has this picture of his fragile mental state been built up across the narrative?

CONSIDER YOUR REACTION . . .
— How did you react to the phone call at the end of the chapter on p. 203? If you haven't read on yet, what do you think is going on?

CHAPTER TWENTY-TWO
SECTION 1 (pp. 204–13)

Focus on: the narrative

ANALYSE . . .
— Look at the description of the gun and the account of Joe practising with it on pp. 205–6. Then read carefully over the description of the handful of soil on p. 207. How might these two passages relate to each other?
— 'He looked down and we exchanged a glance, inverting our usual perspective' (p. 209). What is the larger significance of this remark to the whole of the book?

Focus on: moral questions

WHAT DO YOU THINK? . . .
— Johnny gives Joe two tactical rules: 'Number one, always win, and number two, always cheat' (p. 206). What do you make of this advice? Can you apply it seriously? What would happen if this were to be the way you behaved all the time? How does this advice relate to the themes of the novel as a whole?

CHAPTER TWENTY-TWO
SECTION 2 (pp. 213–15)

Focus on: the theme of the traumatic event

ANALYSE AND COMPARE . . .
— This is the third dramatically shocking event in the novel: the ballooning accident and the shooting in the restaurant being the other two. In what ways does Joe's telling of the events differ on each occasion? In what ways is it the same?
— What happens to time in each of these scenes?

Focus on: the theme of trust

DISCUSS . . .
— Consider why Clarissa is so appalled on pp. 214–15.

CHAPTER TWENTY-THREE
(pp. 216–19)

Focus on: point of view

ASK YOURSELF . . .
— How significant is the fact that this is the very first time in the novel that we have heard Clarissa's own unmediated voice?

RETELL . . .
— Read Clarissa's letter very carefully. Now look back at the account of the ballooning accident in the first chapters and briefly retell the event from Clarissa's point of view. Remember that you may now have much more information about what happened than you had then.

CONSIDER MEANING, MESSAGE AND TONE . . .

— Clarissa writes, 'As far as I was concerned you had nothing to be ashamed of' (p. 217). What exactly does she mean? And what is she suggesting but does not say?

— 'I always thought our love was the kind that was meant to go on and on. Perhaps it will. I just don't know,' writes Clarissa (p. 219). Why is this remark here? What relevance does it have to the novel as a whole? Or to the title of the novel?

CHAPTER TWENTY-FOUR
(pp. 220–31)

Focus on: narrative and storytelling

CONSIDER THE WORD CHOICE AND COMPARE . . .

— Look back at the opening chapters. How many words appear in both places? (Apart from obvious things like 'and' and 'the', of course.) How many scenes and images deriving from the opening chapters are revisited here?

— On p. 224 Clarissa and Rachael share a story about naming. On p. 227 we learn that the two strangers' names – characters introduced very late in the novel – are 'James Reid' and 'Bonnie Deedes'. Put these two passages together and consider their mutual implications. Why are we given the reference to 'guessing your name'? Why is the professor called 'Reid'? Why is his girlfriend 'Bonnie Deedes'? And what does this suggest about our subliminal reaction to the ending of the story?

DISCUSS . . .

— How satisfying is this ending? In how many different ways does it provide a resolution, and to how many different stories? How convinced are you?

APPENDIX I
(pp. 233–43)

Focus on: narrative and language

ANALYSE LANGUAGE AND PLOT . . .

— What effect does this report have on your attitudes to the events you have followed in the novel? Why is this added as an 'Appendix'? How do you, as a reader, react to the coolly academic discussion of the scenes you have witnessed? How close is this account to what you feel you already know? What new information are you offered?

— In what ways does the language of this passage differ from that used in the rest of the book? Remember that Joe Rose is a science writer.

COMPARE . . .

— Read the last chapter (pp. 311–24) of Margaret Atwood's *The Handmaid's Tale* (1985). This is also a 'scientific' and analytical recounting of the events of the novel that goes before, though there the setting is an imagined academic conference taking place some time in the future. In what ways are these two Appendices similar? In what ways are they different?

APPENDIX II
(pp. 244–5)

Focus on: the theme of obsession

DISCUSS . . .

— Why is it the voice of Jed Parry that ends the novel? What difference does this make to your attitude to what went before?

ANALYSE CHARACTERISATION AND LANGUAGE . . .
— How many elements in Jed's letter might remind you of
the ballooning accident that began the whole story? Underline
relevant words and phrases.

Looking over the whole novel

QUESTIONS FOR DISCUSSION OR ESSAYS
1. 'These things bind you together you know, and you have
to talk' (p. 229). Consider the ways in which McEwan uses a
need to 'talk', to tell stories about experience, as a structuring
device in *Enduring Love*.

2. Discuss the theme of forgiveness in the novel.

3. Why is this novel called *Enduring Love?*

4. 'What you see is not what you see. It's who you are.'
Consider this quotation in the light of the way characters are
developed in *Enduring Love*.

5. '*Enduring Love* concludes with a passionate love letter written
by a deluded man and a scientific and rational explanation of
his condition. Both are equally false.' Discuss.

6. Analyse the use of letters (both represented and referred
to) in *Enduring Love*.

Contexts, comparisons and complementary readings

ENDURING LOVE

Focus on: the theme of the 'conflict' between science and religion

COMPARE . . .
— Read Mary Shelley's *Frankenstein* (1818). How is the idea of the rationalist scientific mind set up in opposition to the values of the heart and the domestic scene? In what ways does McEwan's project in *Enduring Love* work out similar ideas to those played out in Shelley's *Frankenstein*?

Focus on: the theme of love

CONSIDER . . .
— 'Love' is used to describe a great variety of feelings, not all of which are easy to define. Do you have a clear idea what you mean when you use this term?
— Brainstorm the word 'love': write it down, and branch out

to as many different kinds of love as you can think of. Now consider which of these kinds might give rise to the most 'enduring love'.

ANALYSE WORD CHOICE AND CREATE . . .

— Jot down the lyrics of as many pop songs as you can think of that are about love. How often is the word used? How many times is it repeated?

— Now write some lyrics for a pop song of your own about love. How do these popular notions of love, and your own, compare? And how do either or both of them relate to the themes of the novel?

COMPARE . . .

— Read a translation of Roland Barthes's *A Lover's Discourse: Fragments* (1977). You don't need to look at all of it, just whichever sections interest you. Why might the subtitle of the book be 'Fragments'? In what ways is this theoretical account of love's processes similar to that in *Enduring Love*? And in what ways is it different?

Focus on: the theme of obsession

ANALYSE VOCABULARY AND COMPARE . . .

In some people certain kinds of love at certain times in their lives can become an obsession. In many ways this is normal, and it can lead to the production of important works of art. Picasso, for instance, painted portraits of Dora Maar over and over again. But there can also be an unhealthy kind of obsession, which is similarly given the name of 'love', even when there is no knowledge of the supposed 'beloved'.

— Read the letter, Letter XCIX, Wedn.s, April 11, 12, from Samuel Richardson's novel *Clarissa* (1747–49).

— How can you tell from the language used that the kind of love displayed here is obsessional? Compare it with one of Jed Parry's letters. In what ways does he use a similar word vocabulary or method of writing?

Focus on: the theme of stalker and victim

SEARCH . . .
— A modern name for a phenomenon that is not necessarily modern is the term 'stalking'. What stories of stalking can you recall from the newspapers? What kind of people get 'stalked'? What do you think this obsession is about? What do you imagine to be the common characteristics of people who are 'stalkers'? In what ways does the characterisation of Jed Parry conform to these?
— What are the characteristics of the genre of 'psychological thriller'? Can you name some examples? What is their attraction for readers? Does the term help to define *Enduring Love*?

COMPARE . . .
— Read either John Fowles's novel *The Collector* or Nigel Williams's novel *Stalking Fiona*. How do either or both of these writers treat the notion of stalking, and how does that compare with the way McEwan handles it?

Focus on: the theme of trust

COMPARE . . .
— Read Thomas Wyatt's poem 'They flee from me that sometyme did me seek' (c. 1535). How can you tell that this is a poem about loss of trust?
— Read the account of Judas's betrayal of Christ in the New

Testament. What is it about these events that makes what happens so painful? Is there any comparable moment in *Enduring Love*?

Focus on: the theme of the disruption of normal, everyday patterns by a strange event

COMPARE . . .

— Where else does this theme occur in McEwan's writings? Read the first chapter of *The Child in Time* or Chapter Nine of *The Comfort of Strangers*. How do those novels compare in their treatment of the theme of disruption of the ordinary?

— Read the article by McEwan published in the *Guardian* on 15 September 2001. He is writing about his own reaction to the attack on the World Trade Center in New York. But in what ways do the themes that he draws out in this article compare with the themes that he uses in *Enduring Love*?

Focus on: the theme of storytelling and point of view

ANALYSE . . .

First-person narratives – which is, for the most part, the main narrative form adopted in *Enduring Love* – always have to be regarded with some suspicion, as we are only given one person's point of view.

— Read the following extract from Lewis Carroll's *Through the Looking-Glass* (1871), Chapter Six, where Alice meets Humpty Dumpty:

'Don't stand chattering to yourself like that,' Humpty Dumpty said, looking at her for the first time, 'but tell me your name and your business.'

'My name is Alice, but —'

'It's a stupid name enough!' Humpty Dumpty interrupted impatiently. 'What does it mean?'

'*Must* a name mean something?' Alice asked doubtfully.

'Of course it must,' Humpty said with a short laugh: '*my* name means the shape I am — and a good handsome shape it is, too. With a name like yours, you might be any shape, almost' ... 'When *I* use a word,' Humpty Dumpty said in a rather scornful tone, 'it means just what I choose it to mean — neither more nor less.'

'The question is,' said Alice, 'whether you *can* make words mean different things.'

'The question is,' said Humpty Dumpty, 'which is to be master — that's all.'

— What is funny about what Humpty Dumpty says about words? How much of his absurd position might actually contain a truth? Find places in *Enduring Love* where characters make words mean what they want them to mean.

VINTAGE
LIVING
TEXTS

Atonement

IN CLOSE-UP

Reading guides for

ATONEMENT

BEFORE YOU BEGIN TO READ . . .
Read the section on *Atonement* from the interview. You will see that McEwan identifies a number of themes and techniques that are discussed in the novel. These include:

- Crime, guilt and punishment
- Storytelling
- War, and the legacy of war
- The treatment of violence
- The creation of character

Other themes that you might like to bear in mind as you read could include:

- Innocence and experience
- Ascribing values
- The idea of the house
- Language and obscenity

Reading activities: detailed analysis

CHAPTER ONE
SECTION I (pp. 3–8)

Focus on: genre and characterisation

DISTINGUISH AND DEFINE . . .

— Analyse the words and phrases used to describe Briony's play on p. 3. What kind of play is it? Choose from these definitions: romantic, satirical, farcical, melodramatic, tragic, experimental, comic.

— Now look at p. 45, where Briony tells Cecilia that her play is the 'wrong genre'. Define what Briony may mean and consider the demands made on the reader by McEwan's narrative method, which sets up a concept in one place, to return to it in another.

— The plot of the play gives us some clues about Briony's character. What does it tell us about her fascination with romance and her need for moral order?

Focus on: narrative technique

ANALYSE . . .

— What sort of world is depicted in this opening section?

What effects are achieved by the narrative viewpoint being that of an intense, imaginative and dramatically inclined young girl?

CHAPTER ONE
SECTION 2 (pp. 8–17)

Focus on: narrative viewpoint

LIST . . .

— Although the narrative of *Atonement* is written in the third person, the viewpoint is mainly Briony's. And yet there are a number of passages in this section, and elsewhere, which suggest a more mature intelligence at work in the judgements that are made (the reason for this will not be explained until the end of the novel). Find examples of comments in which the language or the sentiment seems to derive from a more mature narrative viewpoint than Briony's teenage perspective.

REVISE AND RETELL . . .

— Retell some or all of the events from the Quinceys' arrival to the end of Chapter One, from Lola's point of view. Present the same events in such a way as to make us care more for Lola than for Briony. How important is point of view in this section?

CHAPTER TWO
SECTION 1 (pp. 18–23)

Focus on: sense of place

EXAMINE . . .
— Novels often use a particular setting to create a mood or to reflect on the themes of the story. Consider the description of the Tallis home and grounds in this section. Which details create a sense of place? What might be the symbolic qualities of the house? What values did Harry Tallis, who built the house, wish it to represent? What hints are there in the family history that this was a façade hiding less reassuring truths?

Focus on: the theme of at-one-ment and alienation

CRITICALLY EVALUATE . . .
— The narrative point of view switches to Cecilia in this section, and she is uncomfortable and at odds with her home and family. Pick out the ways in which Cecilia's sense of alienation from the Tallis household is emphasised in this section. Evaluate the importance of Cecilia's alienated perspective here and in the novel as a whole.

CHAPTER TWO
SECTION 2 (pp. 23–31)

Focus on: symbolism

ANALYSE . . .
— Look at what we are told about Uncle Clem's vase, both in this section and on pp. 22–3. Consider the various ways in

which it acts as a symbol. What did it symbolise when it was given to Uncle Clem by the people he saved? What has it come to symbolise to the Tallises in the story they tell of his exploits? Remember that the vase and what happens to it will continue to have symbolic overtones in the ensuing scenes: be alert to these, and to the way McEwan employs them.

Focus on: characterisation

COMMENT ON . . .
— Read the conversation between Cecilia and Robbie on pp. 25–7. This account emphasises a mixture of attraction and antagonism between them. What hints are given to explain this complex play of reactions? Consider the part that social position, influence, intelligence, talent and sexuality might play.

Focus on: reference and allusion

RESEARCH . . .
— On p. 31 we are told about the power of 'the lingering spirit of [Cecilia's] fury'. By implication, this reference in this final section might suggest that Cecilia views herself as one of the Furies – or Erinyes, merciless goddesses of vengeance in Greek and Roman mythology – who punished all wrongdoing. Read up about the Furies in a dictionary of classical mythology. Why might Cecilia's self-casting in this role be seen ironically? What impulses really lie behind Cecilia's 'fury'?

Focus on: the theme of ascribing value

COMPARE . . .
— Read John Keats's poem 'Ode on a Grecian Urn' (1819). Compare and contrast the ways that Keats's urn (or vase, or pot) and the Tallis vase are depicted, the symbolic values that are attributed to them and the different fates of Keats's urn,

which is 'still unravish'd', and the Tallis vase, which (having survived a war) is broken in a petty squabble. What light does this comparison throw on literary symbols, transcendent values and passing passions? How might the image of the shattered 'art object' be played out in the themes of the novel as a whole?

CHAPTER THREE
(pp. 32–42)

Focus on: the theme of crime and punishment

EXAMINE . . .
— Following Robbie's 'crime' of accidentally breaking the vase and Cecilia's punishment, Jackson unwittingly wets his bed and is punished for it. Examine the rationale behind his punishment and the way in which Mrs Tallis's decision is enforced through Betty. In what ways is this small instance of crime and punishment revealing of injustice and hypocrisy in the Tallis household?

Focus on: the theme of life as drama

CONSIDER . . .
— Lola adopts the 'guise' of an adult. How does she betray her self-consciousness in this role?

Focus on: the theme of contrasting perspectives

COMPARE AND CONTRAST . . .
— Briony is disconcerted whenever her 'self-contained world' is challenged by others' needs. Compare her perspective of the Briony–Robbie conversation on pp. 38–9 with Cecilia's view in the previous chapter, and consider how both girls invent what

they see, while believing that what they see is what is really there.

Focus on: the theme of life as fiction

DISCUSS . . .

— Read carefully the paragraph beginning 'Six decades later ...' on p. 41. This is an example of McEwan's (and Briony's) use of prolepsis – a looking forward to a future time disclosing facts that cannot be known at the strict moment in time being portrayed. Discuss what this paragraph suggests about the relationship between truth and stories. Consider also what effect this 'flash-forward' has on your attitude to the story that is unfolding.

CHAPTER FOUR
(pp. 43–54)

Focus on: the theme of ascribing value

DISCUSS . . .

— We learn that Jack Tallis has 'precise ideas about where and when a woman should be seen smoking ... notions as self-evident to him as natural justice'. Consider the effect of the words 'precise' and 'to him' in their contexts. Are etiquette and natural justice linked? Use these quotations as a starting point for discussion:

- 'In halle, in chamber, ore where thou gon,/Nutur and good manners mykth man' – *Urbanitatis, 1490*
- 'It is almost a definition of a gentleman to say that he is one who never inflicts pain' – Cardinal Newman
- 'To some the strict observance of an etiquette may seem

but a manifestation of snobbery' – David Williamson, co-editor, *Debrett's Peerage and Baronetage*

— How significant are ideas of 'appropriate behaviour' to the development of the themes of the novel as a whole?

Focus on: narrative technique

ANALYSE . . .
— Consider how our reactions to Marshall are influenced by the way in which he is presented on pp. 49–54. Look in particular at the effect of his allusions to Hitler, and at how Cecilia's satirical view colours the narrative.

CHAPTER FIVE
(pp. 55–62)

Focus on: the theme of the power of words

— This chapter has many references to words and their ambiguous relationship to truth. Find examples on pp. 57–62 of words that speak the truth, words that conceal the truth, words that break taboo, words as magic talismans, and list them. Critically evaluate the importance of the theme of the power of words in relation to the whole novel.

Focus on: characterisation

ANALYSE . . .
— Examine how Marshall and Lola relate to each other in this chapter. In what ways are they each exposed as dissembling? What apparently motivates them? How do you react to them, and how are your reactions manipulated by the text?

RETELL . . .

— Relate this chapter from Marshall's point of view. Imply his motives (acknowledged or not by him) and indicate his limitations. How self-aware is he?

CHAPTER SIX
(pp. 63–71)

Focus on: narrative viewpoint

CRITICALLY EVALUATE . . .

— 'Only the truth came back to her, for what she knew, she knew . . . She lay in the dark and knew everything' (p. 66). Emily's view of herself as all-knowing and clear-sighted is partly justified, and partly denied by the other perspectives that we are given on what is going on. Analyse the ways in which Emily Tallis creates 'truth' according to her own values just as much as the other characters do.

CHAPTER SEVEN
SECTION I (pp. 72–3)

Focus on: architecture and setting as symbols

DISTINGUISH AND INTERPRET THE IMAGERY . . .

— Write a list of the words that have negative connotations in the description of the temple. These words are descriptive, of course, but they also imply a larger corruption and decay. How do they affect you as a reader?

— What symbolic purpose does the description of the decaying, non-religious 'temple' serve at this point in the novel? How does it relate to the novel as a whole? Consider especially the last line of this description on p. 73. How does this conclusion hint at the themes of the novel?

CHAPTER SEVEN
SECTION 2 (pp. 73–7)

Focus on: characterisation

ASSESS . . .
— Briony loses herself in self-loving reverie, then is recalled to the 'hard mass of the actual' – 'now she was back in the world, not one she could make, but the one that had made her' – in which she feels her 'insignificance' (pp. 76–7). Consider the ways in which her insignificance has been shown to her since the start of the novel. In what ways has Briony matured since that point? In what ways is her world view still childish? Note especially the end of this chapter, where Briony decides to challenge fate and stand still, waiting for the event that will change her for ever. Remember this moment; you will need to come back to it.

CHAPTER EIGHT
SECTION 1 (pp. 78–95)

Focus on: characterisation

LIST AND EVALUATE . . .
— Robbie has been viewed from others' perspectives until now: in this chapter we are given an insight into his thoughts, feelings and attitudes. Analyse what we learn about Robbie from this section.

Focus on: narrative viewpoints

COMPARE . . .

— Contrast Robbie's memory of taking his 'work shoes' off in front of Cecilia with Cecilia's memory of it on p. 27. Now compare Robbie's interpretation that Cecilia had undressed in front of him to 'humiliate him' with Cecilia's view of it as 'reckless, ridiculous, and above all shaming' on p. 107 and her account of her feelings about it to Robbie on p. 134. What do these overlapping perspectives contribute to our sense of a growing diversity of narrative viewpoints? How do we decide which of these is 'reliable' and which 'unreliable'? Bear this question in mind as you read, because it is one that will become very important to your reading of the novel as a whole.

Focus on: characterisation

DEFINE . . .

— Consider the idea of 'freedom', which will become an important theme in this novel. What circumstances are necessary for freedom? Look at the ways in which Robbie thinks of freedom in this passage. In these terms, does any other character enjoy more 'freedom'?

COMPARE . . .

— Read pp. 92–3, where Robbie imagines his future as a doctor, and note the sentence 'He was thinking of the nineteenth-century novel'. In George Eliot's *Middlemarch* (1870–1) Tertius Lydgate is a doctor with similar ambitions, which end up being thwarted both by circumstances and by certain elements of weakness in his own character. McEwan mentions his fondness for *Middlemarch* in the author interview. Read Chapter 15 of Eliot's novel and compare the character and scope of Lydgate's ambitions with those of Robbie.

CHAPTER NINE
(pp. 96–112)

Focus on: characterisation

SUMMARISE AND ASSESS . . .
— Look at Cecilia's preparations in dressing for dinner, her reactions to the twins, her visit to the kitchen, her attitude to her mother and her stream of thoughts. What do all of these reveal about her motives and impulses?

COMPARE AND CONTRAST . . .
— Read the description of Jackson's face at Cecilia's door on p. 99. Here McEwan uses the term 'Picasso-like perspective'. In *Enduring Love* (p. 23) McEwan's narrator uses the phrase 'a radical Picassoesque violation of perspective'. Compare the two moments in each novel. What is McEwan trying to achieve for us by using this allusion to Picasso's abstract technique?

EXAMINE . . .
— Are you surprised by Cecilia's reaction to the letter? What does it reveal about her character?

CHAPTER TEN
(pp. 113–24)

Focus on: the themes of ascribing value and contrasting perspectives

TRACE AND ASSESS THE VOCABULARY . . .
— Briony believes she is 'entering an arena of adult emotion and dissembling'. Read pp. 113–16. How does she try to make sense of what she has learned? The language and imagery that

are used to describe her reaction convey an order of values. Compare and contrast these values with those set up by the images on p. 3.

Focus on: forms of irony

LIST AND ANALYSE WORDS . . .

— Briony inhabits a world somewhere between childhood and adulthood. Which words on pp. 113–16 ironically show her naïveté?

— Look at Briony's conversation with Lola on pp. 116–20. How does the narrative suggest that Lola is not to be trusted, even at a moment when Briony feels sympathy and affection for her?

CHAPTER ELEVEN
SECTION I (pp. 125–30)

Focus on: narrative technique

EXPLAIN . . .

— The first section of Chapter Eleven describes the Tallises' dinner party from various different viewpoints – the first passage to do so. How does this narrative technique convey the distance between what characters say and what they think? Which characters' thoughts are we denied access to, and why might this be significant?

COMPARE . . .

— Read Chapter Seventeen of Virginia Woolf's *To the Lighthouse* (1927), pp. 77–103. How does this account of a dinner party differ from that in *Atonement*? How important is the food served in each? What does it symbolise? How does Mrs

Ramsay's role in the Woolf novel compare with that played by Emily Tallis? What mood is portrayed in each extract?

CHAPTER ELEVEN
SECTION 2 (pp. 130–9)

Focus on: narrative viewpoint

COMPARE . . .
— Contrast the description of Cecilia and Robbie's sexual initiation with the description of Connie and Mellors's first lovemaking in D. H. Lawrence's *Lady Chatterley's Lover* (1928). Consider how both passages stress the paradox of lovers becoming strangers in intimacy, and of the loss of self in the sexual encounter. Compare these descriptions with other attempts by writers to convey sexual ecstasy, such as John Donne's Elegy 19, 'To His Mistress Going to Bed', or Robert Browning's lyric 'Now'.

SEARCH . . .
— 'It is common enough at such times to fantasize arriving in a remote and high place . . .' (p. 138). Whose viewpoint is expressed here? The playfully extended metaphor that follows fits Robbie's love of walking, but this comment suggests a greater experience than Robbie's. Here, as on p. 13, the reader becomes aware of a controlling intelligence behind the narrative, giving it shape and expression. How do we know if we can trust this narrative voice? Read up the entry on 'the unreliable narrator' in the glossary of literary terms, or in David Lodge's *The Art of Fiction*. Or read the section on 'Addresser, Address, Addressee' in Rob Pope's *The English Studies Book* (1998), pp. 160–2.

CHAPTER ELEVEN
SECTIONS 3 AND 4 (pp. 139–44)

Focus on: narrative structure

DISTINGUISH AND DEFINE . . .

— The juxtaposition of Robbie's memories of being with Cecilia and the dinner party emphasise a contrast between passion and protocol that has run throughout the novel. In what ways do Mrs Tallis's bland attempts to keep up etiquette seem inadequate to control the passions that are apparently stirring in all the hearts around the table, except hers?

CHAPTER TWELVE
SECTIONS 1 AND 2 (pp. 145–55)

Focus on: characterisation and the theme of ascribing value

INTERPRET . . .

— What values and attitudes inform Emily Tallis's thoughts? How self-aware is she? Look in particular for examples of conventional attitudes, polite hypocrisy, social myopia and complacency.

— Leon (p. 155), Cecilia (p. 105) and Briony (p. 121) all feel 'obliged to protect her from seeming ineffectual' (p. 128). How does the end of Chapter Twelve change this situation?

— Consider also the picture we are given in this chapter of Jack Tallis's attitudes: towards his wife, towards his work, towards Robbie. What do these contribute to a sense that the stories they tell about their own lives are a distortion of the truth?

CHAPTER THIRTEEN
SECTIONS I AND 2 (pp. 156–72)

Focus on: the theme of life as fiction, life as drama

DISCUSS . . .
— Briony thinks of the 'drama of life' (p. 160). Discuss the relationships between experience, fiction and self-dramatisation in Briony's mind in this section.

Focus on: the setting as symbol

OUTLINE AND INTERPRET . . .
— The crucial conversation with Lola that will determine events hereafter occurs on 'an artificial island in an artificial lake' (p. 163). The island has already featured in the novel, both as a literal part of the grounds and as a symbol for values and states of mind. What does the fact of the artificiality of the island add to its symbolic value at this moment, bearing in mind the emphasis on Briony's impulse to step out of reality into the artifice of the world of the imagination?

Focus on: the theme of the power of words

COMMENT ON . . .
— 'Suddenly, Briony wanted to say his name. To seal the crime, frame it with the victim's curse, close his fate with the magic of naming' (p. 165), and she goes on to name Robbie three times, despite Lola's lack of confirmation. Analyse the language in the quotation above. What does it suggest about how Briony thinks?

REVISE AND RETELL . . .
— What aspects of Lola's response suggest that she is hiding something here? Given recent events in the novel, what do you

think may have occurred on the island? Put your own interpretation on what has happened, then rewrite this scene from
Lola's point of view, explaining why she reacts as she does
when Briony discovers her.

Focus on: the theme of crime, guilt and punishment

DISCUSS AND CONTRAST . . .

— Read the paragraph beginning 'And so their respective
positions . . .' on p. 167. We are told that Briony, in accusing
Robbie, acted 'innocently', and that Lola simply performed
the roles given to her. Discuss this question: if Robbie is innocent, which girl should carry the greater burden of guilt for
his accusation?

EVALUATE . . .

— Assess the paragraphs on pp. 168–71 that explain how
Briony held to a 'truth' based, not on what she saw, but on
what she believed, and how she defended that truth against
others' questions and her own doubts. What exactly is she guilty
of here?

CHAPTER FOURTEEN
(pp. 173–87)

Focus on: characterisation and motive

ANALYSE . . .

— Account for Cecilia's reactions to events in this chapter.
— Consider how Marshall behaves in this chapter.
— Contrast Emily's view of the policemen with their
behaviour.

Focus on: the theme of ascribing value and perspective

ANALYSE . . .
— Assess the symbolic significance of the 'inhuman' shape transforming into Robbie guiding the twins back to safety (p. 182).

SEARCH AND COMPARE . . .
— Read up the story of St Christopher. Or read the parable of the Good Samaritan in the New Testament. How might either or both of these stories suggest symbolic parallels for Robbie's action and character at this moment in the novel? Where – in the novel as a whole – might there be other examples of incidents that also relate to these parables?

TRACE AND RETELL . . .
— Consider Briony's view of Robbie's arrest on pp. 184–6, then rewrite the scene according to your interpretation.
— What do you imagine Cecilia said to Robbie in the presence of the policemen?

PART ONE

Looking over Part One

QUESTIONS FOR DISCUSSION OR ESSAYS
1. Discuss the ways in which characters in the first part of *Atonement* make sense of their lives by telling stories about them.

2. How is the theme of crime and punishment developed in Part One?

3.   Consider the significances of 'innocence' in Part One.

4.   Discuss the use that McEwan makes of contrasting and overlapping narrative points of view in Part One.

5.   'The framework that lies behind each of the characters' values is provided by his or her social identity.' Assess the validity of this claim.

6.   Consider the ways in which McEwan balances the realistic and symbolic effects of the settings of Part One.

7.   What connotations has the title *Atonement* taken on in your reading of the novel?

PART TWO
SECTION 1 (pp. 191–201)

Focus on: contrasting tones

COMPARE AND CONTRAST . . .
— Assess the nature of the shift in tone between Parts One and Two. What causes it?
— Contrast the atmosphere of the meal that Robbie eats with the soldiers with the dinner in Chapter Eleven. Does the latter meal have its own kind of 'etiquette'?

PART TWO
SECTION 2 (pp. 202–13)

Focus on: the theme of life as fiction

ANALYSE . . .
— Prison and separation forced Robbie and Cecilia to communicate for years by letter. What part does storytelling play in their view of their lives and their love affair? We have already seen the precariousness of fantasy in Briony: how is the precariousness of Robbie and Cecilia's 'story' of their love emphasised?

Focus on: the theme of crime, punishment and atonement

DISCUSS . . .
— Examine the ways in which these themes are developed in this section.

PART TWO
SECTION 3 (pp. 214–26)

Focus on: motive

ASSESS . . .
— What needs and impulses bind Robbie, Mace and Nettle together?

DISTINGUISH GENRES . . .
— Analyse the elements of comedy and caricature in the portrayal of the major on pp. 220–3. Is he credible? What motives are being satirised in his portrait, and how are they made ridiculous?

Focus on: characterisation

COMMENT ON . . .

— Consider the characters of Mace and Nettle. What suggestions are there that they are not as harsh as they appear?

CONSIDER AND COMPARE . . .

— Assess the names of characters in this novel. Can you think of names that suggest aspects of the characters to whom they belong? What do the names 'Mace' and 'Nettle' suggest? Now think of other characters' names. McEwan often gives his characters ordinary names with implied connotations.

— Now think back to Emily Tallis, and her preoccupation with etiquette over morality or feeling. In what ways do Mace and Nettle throw her values into relief?

PART TWO
SECTION 4 (pp. 226–34)

Focus on: the theme of perspectives and ascribing value

ANALYSE . . .

— Punishment, forgiveness, atonement, redemption: assess what we know of Robbie's, Cecilia's, Briony's, Emily's and Jack's attitudes to these subjects at this stage in the novel.

COMPARE AND CONTRAST . . .

— 'I love you' (p. 232). Compare Briony's declaration of these words to Robbie with the way Cecilia is presented as speaking (we assume) the same words on p. 137. What value does Robbie put on these words when spoken by each of the two girls?

— Robbie re-interprets the events of the evening he was

arrested in the light of the conviction that Briony harboured unrequited love for him. Now turn to p. 342, where an older Briony recalls of Robbie 'the memory of a passion she'd had for him, a real crush that had lasted days. Then she confessed it to him one morning in the garden and immediately forgot about it.' They are both re-inventing the past. Whose version of the story can we trust? Either? Both? Neither?

PART TWO
SECTION 5 (pp. 234–46)

Focus on: narrative technique

SEARCH AND COMPARE . . .
— This section contains many striking juxtapositions: of the mundane with the extraordinary; of details that 'make sense' with those that defy it; of honourable and shameful actions. How does this narrative technique contribute to your impressions of the experience of war and of the values that prevail in war?

IMAGINE AND RETELL . . .
— '. . . he would track down his father, or his dead father's story – either way, he would become his father's son' (p. 242). Write the 'story' of your own father or mother, and explain how far you are (or are not) your parent's child. How does this telling and retelling of the stories of parents and their children relate to the themes of the novel as a whole?

PART TWO
SECTION 6 (pp. 246–65)

Focus on: the theme of atonement

COMPARE . . .

— As Robbie reaches the crowds at the shore, 'private initiative' is subsumed into the group instinct. Consider the incident of the group victimisation of the RAF man on pp. 250–4, which recalls the victimisation of Robbie that Cecilia ascribed to class resentment (p. 209). What challenge does this incident put to Robbie, Mace and Nettle?

— Now read Act III, scene 7 of Shakespeare's *King Lear*, in which Gloucester is tortured by Lear's daughter Regan and her husband. Compare Mace's action with that of the servants who go to Gloucester's help during and after the torture. In what sense can such individual acts of kindness and bravery be said to 'atone for' violence and cruelty?

PART TWO

Looking over Part Two

QUESTIONS FOR DISCUSSION OR ESSAYS

1. What new connotations has the title *Atonement* taken on in the second part of the novel?

2. Questions of guilt, innocence and redemption in Robbie's personal story are eclipsed by the enormity of the collective guilt of war. Look over Part Two to identify individual acts that imply innocence or guilt, and discuss whether – during a war – individuals retain responsibility for their actions.

3. Consider the significance of separation and unity in Part Two.

4. In what ways do the events of Part Two throw a new light on the events of Part One?

PART THREE
SECTION I (pp. 269–77)

Focus on: narrative shape

IDENTIFY AND DEFINE . . .
— It's 1940 and Briony is eighteen. Because 'the model behind this process was military' (p. 276), there are numerous parallels between Briony's experience as a nurse and Robbie's military experiences at a similar time. Identify them. What might be the symbolic significance of these parallels?

Focus on: characterisation and motive

CONSIDER . . .
— Why has Briony gone into nursing?

Focus on: the theme of perspectives and ascribing value

COMPARE . . .
— Contrast the anger that Briony's errors of deportment elicit from her superiors (pp. 270–1) with the lieutenant's reaction to the corporal's untied laces (p. 246) and with Emily Tallis's reaction to breaches of etiquette (pp. 139–40). Note how context and narrative points of view influence our interpretations of these incidents. Are there other passages in the novel as a whole that set up similar discrepancies between the notions of 'value' held by different characters?

PART THREE
SECTION 2 (pp. 277–82)

Focus on: the theme of innocence and experience

ANALYSE . . .
— How does this section convey a sense of how Briony has changed since Part One? What images of change and loss contribute to the impression of time's effects?

Focus on: narrative technique

RESEARCH AND COMPARE . . .
'The novel of the future would be unlike anything in the past' (p. 282). Briony has been impressed by her reading of Virginia Woolf. An inventively experimental writer, Woolf employed and refined the narrative technique generally known as 'stream of consciousness', which strives to convey the quality of characters' subjective experience, their thoughts, sensations, emotions, memories and fantasies.
— Read Virginia Woolf's essay 'Modern Fiction' (1919). How do Briony's reflections on fictional representation, as mediated through Woolf, invite comparison with McEwan's own techniques?

PART THREE
SECTION 3 (pp. 282–6)

Focus on: ascribing value

DISCUSS . . .
— Briony thinks that 'she would never undo the damage. She was unforgivable' (p. 285). Does the second statement follow

logically from the first, in your view? According to Christian teaching, Christ atoned for human sinfulness by his suffering and death. Consider the details that suggest – literally or symbolically – the absence of Christian belief in the Tallis family, such as the 'temple' that was built 'to enhance the pastoral ideal, and had of course no religious purpose at all' (p. 72), or Leon's 'short, suspended grace', which stops after 'For what we are about to receive' (p. 126). How significant a theme is lack of religious faith in the novel?

PART THREE
SECTION 4 (pp. 287–315)

Focus on: the theme of crime and punishment

ANALYSE . . .

— 'Her secret torment and the public upheaval of war had always seemed separate worlds, but now she understood how the war might compound her crime' (p. 288). Consider again the main themes that were developed on a 'private' level in the isolated world of the Tallis household in Part One: innocence lost; crime and guilt; ascribing value; atonement and alienation; social identity; life as fiction. How have these themes been developed on a 'public' level in Parts Two and Three? In what ways is the narrative beginning to link the two arenas of private and public?

Focus on: the theme of life as fiction

EXAMINE AND ASSESS . . .

— It is clear from the letter from the editor of *Horizon* that the story Briony submitted was based on the experiences narrated in Part One. Consider the extent to which the narrative of Part One of *Atonement* follows the advice in the editor's letter. What does this suggest about who narrates the novel? 'C.C.' is an allusion to Cyril Connolly, who edited a real magazine called *Horizon* from 1939 to 1950. What does this blurring of the boundaries between 'real life' and 'fiction' contribute to the theme in the novel of life as fiction?

PART THREE
SECTION 5 (pp. 315–27)

Focus on: the theme of crime, guilt and punishment

ANALYSE AND INTERPRET THROUGH CLOSE READING . . .
On p. 324 the narrative states that it was Marshall who raped Lola. This idea has been hinted at earlier, but its confirmation here leads the reader to re-evaluate some earlier scenes:

- Reread the episode of Lola's first meeting with Paul Marshall in the nursery on pp. 60–2. Look particularly at the references to Marshall's sisters, to Lola's clothes, and at his reaction to Lola eating the Amo chocolate bar.
- Reread the account of the dinner party in Chapter Eleven (pp. 125–30) and re-interpret Marshall's behaviour, Lola's injury and the twins' escape in the light of the knowledge that Marshall later raped Lola.
- Reread the description of the aftermath of Lola's rape in Chapter Fourteen, and re-interpret Marshall's behaviour on that occasion (especially on p. 175).

— In a retrospective reading these scenes are ironic, since we are now aware of the distance between Marshall's outward behaviour and what he has done. 'Proleptic' irony derives its effect from narrative developments that have not yet happened. It is therefore understood only in retrospect. How does this late re-evaluation of earlier scenes fit the novel's overall theme of contrasting perspectives?

EXAMINE, INTERPRET AND ASSESS . . .

— Between Chapter Fourteen and the news that Marshall and Lola are marrying on p. 285, Marshall almost slips out of view. There are only two glancing references to his Amo bars (on pp. 239 and 304) to remind us of his existence. Now, suddenly, this minor character takes on major significance in the novel's thematic framework. Consider these questions:

● If Briony's crime was to embellish the truth to suit her view of Robbie, what was Marshall's crime? And what was Lola's?
● How do you react to the fact that Marshall and Lola still enjoy a freedom – from punishment, from shame – that is denied to both Robbie and Briony?
● Briony accused Robbie; Cecilia accused Danny Hardman; no one suspected Marshall. What influence might social position have had on these accusations?

— Briony feels the need 'to proclaim in public all the private anguish' in order to 'purge herself of all that she had done wrong' (p. 325). Consider the validity of the claim that she has never grown out of self-dramatisation.

Focus on: the theme of atonement

ACCOUNT FOR . . .

— Examine and define the ironies implicit in the scene of the Marshalls' marriage. This is the first scene in the narrative to take place in a religious building. The marriage union recalls their sexual encounter by the pagan temple on the island. Briony's desire for forgiveness and atonement contrasts with the Marshalls' apparent lack of shame as they receive the Church's blessings for their 'at-one-ment'. How do you react to this ironic situation?

PART THREE
SECTION 6 (pp. 328–49)

Focus on: narrative technique

DESCRIBE . . .
— Read the scenes between Cecilia, Briony and Robbie, paying attention to the narrative point of view. How is the narrative technique used to emphasise the alienation between Briony and the other two?

Focus on: narrative viewpoint

ANALYSE AND REASSESS . . .
The word 'atonement' is used for the first time in the novel on p. 349. The reader's realisation that the narrative *is* Briony's atonement for her crime against Robbie forces a sudden re-evaluation of it. If, before this point, we had regarded the narrative viewpoint as omniscient, now we might see it as partial. Our trust in the 'authority' of the narrative and in the implied judgements that the narrative has made (consider the portrayal of Emily Tallis, for instance) seem misplaced once we know that the 'author' is Briony, who is implicated in the action as guilty of being a fantasist. Perhaps we might suspect Briony of self-justification, and wonder if she has distorted the truth to exonerate herself.
— How does it affect our reading of Robbie's experiences in Part Two, if we recall that Briony has told them, and that she has never got closer to war than a hospital ward? And what

do we now make of other events at which Briony was not present: the love-making between Robbie and Cecilia, for instance, or the argument by the fountain that Briony witnessed only from a distance? Is Marshall guilty after all, or is that another of Briony's stories? By introducing an element of instability into the narrative viewpoint, McEwan foregrounds again the theme of life as fiction. How are we to distinguish truth from ways of seeing?

PART THREE

Looking over Part Three

QUESTIONS FOR DISCUSSION OR ESSAYS

1. Discuss the implications of the idea that Briony is the author of the narrative as a whole.

2. Compare Robbie and Cecilia as they appear in Part Three with their characterisations earlier in the novel. How have they changed, and what might be the significance of these changes?

3. Consider the significance of alienation and at-one-ment in Part Three of the novel, and the relation of this theme to the novel as a whole.

4. 'The narrative technique of *Atonement* portrays thought, perceptions, sensations, the private consciousness of individual minds, unable to communicate fully with others.' Discuss.

157

PART FOUR
SECTION I (pp. 353–70)

Focus on: the theme of memory

ACCOUNT FOR AND ANALYSE . . .

— Your own experience of the novel means that you too now possess layers of 'memory' across different periods, settings and developing characterisation. Think back and compare your reactions and feelings when reading earlier sections with your perspective on the novel now.

COMPARE . . .

— Read Craig Raine's poem 'The Onion, Memory' (1978). How does his portrayal of the functions of memory compare with McEwan's treatment of the theme of memory?

RESEARCH . . .

— How many popular songs can you think of with the word 'memory' or 'memories' in their lyrics? What do these songs say about memory? Why is it such a potent force in our lives? In what ways are these popular versions of the theme of memory connected to McEwan's deployment of the theme in *Atonement*?

Focus on: the theme of life as fiction

EXPLAIN AND EVALUATE . . .

— 'I've always liked to make a tidy finish' (p. 353). How does this comment set up expectations for the final part of the novel? Which remarks in Part Four keep alive our sense that the account we are reading may not be totally in line with the truth?

CONTRAST . . .

— Look back at the pages that dealt with the genre of Briony's play *The Trials of Arabella* (pp. 3 and 45). 'If I really cared so much about facts, I should have written a different kind of book' (p. 360). How does this section on Briony's fiction compare thematically to the play she wrote as a teenager? What kind of book has Briony written now?

— 'She was always the superior older girl, one step ahead of me. But in that final important matter, I will be ahead of her' (p. 361). Consider the idea that the whole narrative has been informed by an attempt by Briony to win against Lola. Is this interpretation credible? What supports it and what refutes it?

COMPARE . . .

— Read McEwan's *Enduring Love* or Margaret Atwood's *The Handmaid's Tale* (1986). Both of these novels have 'factual' epilogues that mirror, distort or undercut what has gone before. Compare the technique employed in either of those two novels with the conclusion to *Atonement*.

Focus on: the theme of atonement

DISCUSS . . .

— Consider whether it is possible for a man who carries a guilt like Marshall's to make 'amends' (p. 357) by public acts of charity.

PART FOUR
SECTION 2 (pp. 370–2)

Focus on: the theme of life as fiction

COMPARE . . .

— Despite her attempts to create a happy ending, this ending is framed within Briony's darkening despair, her inevitable slide into oblivion. The story she has told is a fight against forgetfulness. Read Dylan Thomas's poem 'Do not go gentle into that good night', and compare his sentiments on the imminent death of his father with Briony's refusal to die without first taking a stand against life's indifference to individual fates.

Focus on: the theme of atonement

DISCUSS . . .

— 'Atonement is an impossibility without a belief in God.' Consider the validity of this statement in the light of Briony's comments on p. 371 in the paragraph 'The problem these fifty-nine years . . . The attempt was all.'

PART FOUR

Looking over Part Four

QUESTIONS FOR DISCUSSION OR ESSAYS

1. '*Atonement* is a pessimistic novel.' Do you agree?

2. Discuss the significance of memory in Part Four of the novel.

3. What effects does McEwan achieve by setting the final part of the novel in contemporary times?

PART FOUR

Longer comparative responses

QUESTIONS FOR ESSAYS OR DISCUSSION

1. Charles Dickens faced a quandary about how to end *Great Expectations* (1860–1): should he end it happily, or should he keep the ending true to the moral lesson that the novel was offering? Should he satisfy his readers' emotional wishes or their sense of moral order? The Penguin edition reproduces both endings, with a commentary. Read them. The choice facing Briony is much less stable, since she implies that the way events really turned out defies a belief in any order, and shows that life and suffering are meaningless and that atonement is not possible. In the interview with McEwan he discusses the ways in which the nineteenth-century realist novel influenced his own work. But the comparison of Dickens with McEwan highlights the loss of a sustaining belief in a moral order that is reflected in contemporary literature. What might have caused this loss? And in what ways does it inform your reading of *Atonement*?

2. Read E. M. Forster's *A Passage to India* (1924). Compare the ways in which McEwan and Forster present the alleged sexual assaults perpetrated in each book, and the fallout from the accusations that are made. How much does the reader know for certain in each case?

3. Read a translation of Alexander Pushkin's poem *Eugene Onegin* (1828), listen to Piotr Tchaikovsky's opera of the same name (1879) or see the film directed by Martha Fiennes (1999). Compare the

juxtaposition that happens in both Pushkin's Tatyana and McEwan's Briony between the attitude of a young girl in the first part and the presentation of her older self in the later part.

4. Read Virginia Woolf's *Mrs Dalloway* (1925), Elizabeth Bowen's *The Death of the Heart* (1938) or Rosamond Lehmann's *Dusty Answer* (1927). In what ways might Briony's development as a novelist be influenced by the work of these other (real) writers and their styles?

5. Read Jane Austen's *Northanger Abbey* (1818), especially Chapters Five and Fourteen, where the narrator considers what novels are and why they might have value. In what ways might Jane Austen's ideas about the novel set out some of the attitudes that are implied either in *Atonement* itself or in the novels that Briony is supposed to have written in the course of the novel as a whole?

Looking over the whole novel

QUESTIONS FOR ESSAYS OR DISCUSSION

1. 'Once broken, never mended'. Discuss, in relation to the imagery and themes of *Atonement*.

2. Consider the importance of Briony's play 'The Trials of Arabella' to the structure of the novel as a whole.

3. In what ways is *Atonement* a meditation on the power of words?

4. Discuss the idea of the country house in *Atonement*.

5. There are three episodes concerning Lola and Paul Marshall in *Atonement*. Assess their significance in relation to the novel as whole.

6. 'Come back' is what Cecilia used to say to Briony as a child when she tried to comfort her sister after a bad dream. How might this particular phrase relate to the themes of the novel?

7. Look back at the end of Chapter Seven on pp. 76–7 and reread the section from 'In a spirit of mutinous resistance . . .' to '. . . and dispelled her insignificance'. How has Briony's 'challenge' to fate been played out in the novel? Does it make any difference that we now know that Briony is the author of the whole narrative?

8. How does the literary concept of 'genre' and its appropriateness to chosen themes inform the novel as a whole?

9 How are Briony's fascination with romance and need for moral order portrayed in the novel as a whole?

Contexts, comparisons and complementary readings

ATONEMENT

Focus on: the theme of innocence and experience

RESEARCH . . .

— *Atonement* shares the theme of the loss of innocence with many novels. Examples that have elements in common with *Atonement* are D. H. Lawrence's *Sons and Lovers* (1913), James Joyce's *Portrait of the Artist as a Young Man* (1914–15), L. P. Hartley's *The Go-Between* (1953), Alice Walker's *The Color Purple* (1982) and Jeanette Winterson's *Oranges Are Not the Only Fruit* (1985). Read one of these novels in whole or in part, consider the ways in which 'rites of passage' are portrayed in the novel and compare it with the way the same themes are developed in Ian McEwan's *Atonement*.

Focus on: the theme of crime, guilt and punishment

DISCUSS . . .

— Look at the list below. These 'crimes' vary greatly in seriousness. Relate these crimes to the events in *Atonement*. Not everyone who commits them in the novel is punished. Invent a punishment that you think is fitting for each one.

- A married man has a long-standing adulterous affair
- A couple who are arguing accidentally break a valuable item belonging to someone else
- A child of nine who is emotionally distressed wets his bed
- A young woman smokes in the house, against her absent father's wishes
- A child is rude to someone at the dinner table
- An unmarried man has consensual sex with an unmarried woman in secret
- A woman falsely accuses a man of a rape, and sees that person go to jail for several years
- A man kills his enemy in wartime
- A man stands by and watches while a mob beats an innocent person to death
- Someone lets another man go to jail for a crime he himself committed.

COMPARE . . .

— Arthur Miller's play *The Crucible* (1953) traces how, from one dissembling girl's self-serving accusations, dire consequences ensue for a seventeenth-century New England community. Compare Lola's character with that of Abigail Williams; and compare the role of Briony, caught up in a process that is 'moving fast and well beyond her control', with that of Mary Warren in Miller's play.

Focus on: the theme of the house

COMPARE . . .

— Read Jane Austen's *Mansfield Park* (1814) Charles Dickens's *Bleak House* (1852–3) or E. M. Forster's *Howards End* (1910). Analyse the descriptions of Mansfield Park, Chesney Wold or Howards End in each book. Consider how those settings contribute to the themes of the book, and compare those writers' techniques with that used by McEwan to depict the Tallis family home as he relates the setting to his themes.

RESEARCH . . .

— Visit Dennis Severs's house at 18 Folgate Street, Spitalfields, London E1. In it Severs created, through objects, the story of an imaginary family who had lived there from the eighteenth century to just after the First World War, when all that remained of the Jervis family were two maiden aunts. The house is now run by the Spitalfields Trust and you can get more information at www.dennissevershouse.co.uk. Or you could read Dennis Severs's book *18 Folgate Street: The Tale of a House in Spitalfields* (2001).

— How can a house both transform us and be transformed by time? Consider how we may change a house, but how the house may also change us. Consider too the fact that the house is likely to last longer. As you read *Atonement*, compare the stories about the rooms and places in 18 Folgate Street with the places, rooms and stories told about the Tallis house.

Focus on: the theme of language and obscenity

— What makes a word obscene? Or is a word not necessarily obscene in itself, but only in context – so that obscenity depends either (or both) on the intention behind the use of the word or (and) on the way it is received?

DEFINE . . .
— Write down the two most obscene English words you can think of — the most offensive words you can use to describe someone. What have you written? What does it say about social attitudes to these things or actions that they are considered terms of the rudest abuse?
— If you, or any of your friends, speak another language, what words are used as abuse in that language? Write them down. Do these obscenities reveal any similar or contrasting attitudes?

Focus on: the theme of war and the legacy of war

RESEARCH . . .
— The Second World War has been so much written about and filmed that for many of us it is hard to separate fact from stories in our understanding of it. Read an historical account of the British retreat to Dunkirk and the evacuations of May/June 1940, and compare this with the fictional account of Part Two. Discuss the area of overlap between storytelling and history telling. Read the section on 'Narrative in History, Novels, News and Film' in Rob Pope's *The English Studies Book*, pp. 206–12.

Focus on: the theme of storytelling

COMPARE . . .
— Compare the alternative endings of *Atonement* with those

offered in John Fowles's novel *The French Lieutenant's Women* (1969). In both cases one ending is conventionally 'happy', the other 'unhappy', and the reader is asked to choose between them. Fowles's novel suggests that the 'happy' ending of the kind that Victorian novelists felt under pressure to provide was inauthentic, whereas modern taste is for an ending that reflects the openness of experience. Which ending of *Atonement* is more satisfying to the reader, in your opinion?

Reference

Selected extracts from reviews

These brief extracts from contemporary reviews of the novels are designed to be used to suggest angles on the text that may be relevant to the themes of the books, or to their settings, their literary methods and their historical contexts, or to indicate their relevance to issues, questions or problems today.

Sometimes one reviewer's opinion will be entirely contradicted by another's. You might use these passages to ask yourself whether or not you agree with the writer's assessments. Or you may take phrases from these reviews to use in framing questions – for discussion, or for essays – about the texts.

Remember, though, three things about newspaper reviews. They are often written under pressure; they have to give the reader some idea of what the book under discussion is like, so they do tend to give space to summarising the plot; and a reviewer's attitude when judging a book that is new in the world – that is, before some received critical consensus has been reached – can sometimes seem, in retrospect, astonishingly naïve, blinkered or over-enthusiastic.

None of these critical opinions represents the last word. They are simply contributions to a cultural debate. As such, they should be approached with intellectual interest – because they can give the mood and tone of a particular time – and they should be treated with suspicion – because the very fact of that prevailing mood and time may distort a clear reading.

THE CHILD IN TIME

Eileen Battersby, 23rd August 1997
From the *Irish Times*
On its tone of 'helplessness'

Ian McEwan is at his most comfortable and convincing when describing strange states of mind. Yet it is interesting that although his career began in the sinister mood of the macabre which dominated his first book, the short-story collection, *First Love, Last Rites* (1975), its successor *In Between the Sheets* (1978), and his first novel, *The Cement Garden*, also published in 1978, and *The Comfort of Strangers* (1981), McEwan has shifted away from the grotesque extremes and has instead become concerned with disturbed and disturbing psychological trauma.

In *The Child in Time* (1987) – his best work to date – the protagonist has to live with the fact that he lost his small daughter in a supermarket. Far more powerful than his previous books, *The Child in Time* is deceptively understated and achieves a sense of quiet helplessness.

Peter Kemp, 7th September 1997
From *The Sunday Times*
On McEwan's themes of children and childhood

Being at risk is something McEwan has always written powerfully about and never with more edge and urgency than here. His early novels and stories, from *First Love, Last Rites* (1975) to *The Comfort of Strangers* (1981), aimed to induce jitters by a narrative calmness macabrely at odds with the alarming events recounted. Calculated unfeelingness was the keynote. As hideous scenarios closed in around endangered innocents, an unnervingly affectless tone chimed in with a prevailing gothic gruesomeness. Children, in particular, were shadowed by threat in McEwan's first books – a situation that persisted into the far more mature, emotionally responsive and responsible novels he began to write with *The Child in Time* at the end of the 1980s. The jeopardised youngster in the balloon's basket at the opening of *Enduring Love* dramatically resurrects this motif along with another that always engages McEwan: the relationship between parents and children, the need to sustain a mutually valuable rapport between the mature and the childlike. Tampered-with children were prominent in his callowly sensational early books. Later, tampered-with, childhoods – ways in which people (such as Jed) can be warped by their upbringing – swivel to the fore. Besides the imperilled boy in the balloon, two other menaced juveniles, the son and daughter of the man killed in the accident, appear here in a sub-plot that provides a variant display of the pains and strains and resiliences of love. Clarissa's unhappiness at her inability to have children – explored with the crisp delicacy that has been such a welcome addition to McEwan's emotional gamut in recent years – tangles into her resentment at what she feels are Joe's excessive demands for her support.

ENDURING LOVE

From *GQ*, October 1997

Ian McEwan's literary career has been rather frustrating. Since his emergence in the Seventies with the creepy domestic Gothic short stories of *In Between the Sheets* – his books have got denser, longer and more aggressively 'literary'. But better? Not really. Take *Enduring Love*. The opening sequence, in which a hot air balloon falls from the sky and tragedy ensues, is wonderful and would make a gripping short story – but from then on the novel meanders. For all McEwan's dabbling in fashionable notions of the philosophy of science, the rest of the book never really adds anything to the strangeness of the first chapter, and ends up as an overwritten psychological thriller.

Dave Barry, 31st October 1997
From the *Manchester Evening News*

Enduring Love, by Ian McEwan (Jonathan Cape, £15.99) is an extraordinary tale of a relationship triggered after a chance meeting in a field. Joe Rose, a science writer, seems to have the perfect existence until religious maniac Jed Parry enters his life. The book explores the paranoia and alienation felt by the victim of a stalker, and the terrible and dramatic consequences which follow. A good read, pacey and exciting at times, but marred by an excessively intellectual style.

From *New Woman*, September 1997

Fans of McEwan will be anticipating the publication of his latest novel, but they may be disappointed by the paucity of the material.

The narrator, Joe Rose, meets Jed Parry as they join the rescuers at a catastrophic ballooning accident. Parry feels that his meeting with Joe is a portent of the great love that should, well, balloon between them. Joe finds Parry ludicrous, ominous and finally frightening. In centring the novel around erotic delusions or 'erotomania', McEwan hopes to stir the currents of pathology and unease as he's done in the past. But so slight is his story that it all has to be supported by a lengthy appendix and case history from the *British Review of Psychiatry*.

Ra Page, 19th December 1997
On the treatment of the theme of science

The key text in this scientific renaissance is Ian McEwan's *Enduring Love* (Cape, £15.99). Instead of just injecting the plot with doses of research and technology, McEwan has actually produced a novel of scientific ideas, a story that addresses consciousness, memory and altruism in a scientific way. Narrated by a science-journalist, Joe Rose, it opens with a bizarre but beautifully constructed ballooning accident in which the failure of Joe and four other helpers to risk their lives results in the death of the bravest among them. The incident triggers a pathological obsession in one of the helpers, Jed Parry, for Joe whom he begins to stalk. What is so remarkable about this novel is the

175

fine balance it strikes between the narrator's personal experiences and his scientific understanding of them.

When it comes to the pertinence of science in literature, McEwan is categorical. 'Even if we leave aside technology,' he stresses, 'science is relevant to the novelist in as much as it explains ourselves to ourselves.' McEwan is characteristically precise about how the novelist can employ science. 'There are two ways you can go,' he explains. 'One is to raid science, especially physics, for its metaphors, which is something we've all done since science found its feet in the 17th century. The other is to wait until science has something profound to say about ourselves; which is what has begun to happen in the biological sciences.

'Obviously, there are limits as to how far we can use science in describing the minutiae of human experience. But those limits are not as great as we once thought.'

For those who aren't as familiar with science as McEwan, the Romantic distrust lingers on. Readers and critics remain precious about who should handle the delicacies of human nature and who shouldn't, and McEwan's novel has been criticised for having too meticulous a narrative voice. It is a criticism which not only overlooks the dynamic of the novel but implies that only non-scientists make for good narrators.

What McEwan's character, Joe Rose, actually offers us is evidence of the suitability of scientific perspectives to the task of narration. Joe's encyclopaedic background knowledge illuminates the prose, widens the context and symbolism of each experience and most importantly isolates him from his immediate environment. As Joe attempts to read his way out of the stalker problem, becoming increasingly convinced by his initial diagnosis, the police and his partner Clarissa, who see no evidence of the harassment, begin to doubt his sanity. Joe's diagnostic rationalism may cost him his intimacy with Clarissa, but it is never inaccurate or inappropriate.

Margaret Lewis, 12th September 1997
From the *Newcastle Journal*
On the treatment of the theme of science

The least happy aspect of what is nevertheless a highly accomplished novel is the overlay of popular science that Joe uses to interpret the world around him.

Is McEwan trying too hard to hitch himself to a fashionable credo? In this novel he flaunts his intelligence and controls his reader with considerable style.

Amanda Craig, 5th September 1997
From the *New Statesman*
On the treatment of the themes of science and rationalism

Jed, as Joe comes to realise, has 'de Clerambault's syndrome', an erotomaniac state in which the subject has the intense delusional belief that the object of their passion is in love with them. Tragic for both sufferer and victim, the syndrome mimics real love although the victim has usually never met the sufferer, or done so only briefly. This is a novel idea, and one which gives rise to many trains of thought on love – was Dante, for instance, a sufferer? – few of which are taken up. What McEwan seems intent on doing is showing how deranged Jed is, and by extension, Christianity. Joe is a successful science writer; his mind is a cornucopia of rationalist arguments, including one (unacknowledged by the author) lifted straight from Harold Bloom on the authorship of the Old Testament. Presented with the outpourings of a born-again nut, 'generally aligned to the culture of personal growth and fulfilment', he reacts as many feel like doing: he reaches for a gun. *Middlemarch* to *Brazzaville Beach* novelists have mined science for metaphor and, perhaps, intellectual respectability. The trouble is, most of us have now read the same books, and we are not overly excited by having rationalist arguments repeated at third-hand in a work of fiction.

Michèle Roberts, 23rd August 1997
From *The Times*
On the theme of men and women

Ian McEwan is always described as writing about gore and nastiness, perverse philosophies, machismo metaphysics – and very fed up he must get with this, too. Just because he once wrote a story about things that go bump in bell-jars doesn't mean he should be typecast for ever as baddish and laddish. In fact, his novels are sheep in wolves' clothing.

Under their dark, bristling, thrillerish surfaces lurk explorations of the way we love now: men and women mostly, but parents and children too. His world appears a naturalistic one, but is also metaphorical, as in a romance. He illuminates inner states as well as outer ones, though his landscapes are always realistic and *noir*-ish enough to satisfy the butchest of readers.

A constant image recurring in his work is the man-woman couple so tightly tangled together and at the same time so confused about sexual difference that an act of violence by a third party is required to allow the protagonists to separate ...

Enduring Love explores the either or thinking that Charlotte Brontë would have recognised. It pits science against madness, man against woman, reason against intuition, rationality against religion, passion against sanity, love against hate. Joe thrashes around in the midst of all these ...

One of the problems is that Jed's homoerotic obsession with Joe is sublimated into the language of religious devotion. He believes he has been chosen by God to draw Joe to the everlasting bliss of the Father's arms. Joe can't see it this way. Having done his homework, he concludes that Jed is suffering from what psychologists have labelled de Clerambault's syndrome. So they can't communicate with each other, because they talk different languages!

Jed represses his homosexual urges and Joe denies that he has any. Jed's love for God and for Joe is presented as the stuff of purest craziness: belief in something that isn't there. Joe has to face the fact that he doesn't, for all his scientific approach to life, understand loving a woman either. It's a skill he's taken for granted. He can't talk to Clarissa about what's happening, partly because she's too busy and tired, partly because she begins to suspect him of being fascinated by Jed. Their relationship, at first apparently so trusting, intimate and strong, shatters under the impact of their inability to support each other.

The novel reaches a satisfying violent denouement after a lovely comic set piece on how to buy a gun from braindead hippies wrecked on too much dope, karma and burnt toast. The princess is rescued from the dragon, even if she goes on criticising the prince for insisting on doing it his way.

I decided that everything really was Clarissa's fault. If authors are still allowed intentions. I think McEwan meant us to be sympathetic to her. But to me she came across as the kind of radical feminist who believes that womanliness will save the world, that women are morally superior to men, that men can't understand feelings. Boy, are those women trouble. They just don't stand by their men.

Alain de Botton, 5th September 1997
From the *Daily Mail*
On the theme of men and women

It would be foolish to give away more of the plot than this, but suffice to say that McEwan is never predictable and keeps up the tension to the last page of this short book. McEwan is fascinated by the fragility of relationships and the difficulties men and women have in talking to each other.

There is a devastating argument scene which shows the ease with which two mature adults can slide into the most childish behaviour which they regret even as the argument unfolds, and yet are helpless to avoid.

Nicholas Royle, 17th September 1997
From *Time Out*
On narrative point of view and the theme of
men and women

In *Enduring Love*, Ian McEwan offers the reader the most insightful and penetrating dissection of an argument between husband and wife that I can remember. It's an argument which tugs at the first threads of a marriage which threatens to unravel, and McEwan's approach to it is particularly interesting for his narrator's switch to see it from his wife's point of view.

If it weren't for de Clérambault sufferer Jed Parry, the argument between Joe and Clarissa would never have taken place. Following a ballooning incident in which Parry and Joe witness a man's death, Parry becomes obsessed with Joe, convinced that the older man is in love with him and that it is his duty to bring Joe to God. Clarissa fails to take Parry's threat as seriously as Joe would like her to and even wonders if her husband is perhaps overreacting to a harmless young man.

The pleasure for the reader lies partly in the fact that we know he is not overreacting and that things are going to get worse before they get better – if indeed they get better at all. Over the course of the novel, the author is perhaps a little unfair to the Clarissa character.

Adam Mars-Jones, 5th September 1997
From the *Observer*
On narrative and unreliability

There's an odd moment in Ian McEwan's new novel, when the narrator, Joe Rose, is being interviewed by the police after a murder attempt in a restaurant. Asked what flavour of ice cream he was eating before the shooting, he replies: 'Apple'. It's not simply that this goes against the testimony of other witnesses, who remember the attack occurring fractionally earlier – the sorbets tainted with blood before they could reach the lunchers who had ordered them – but it contradicts the version we were given earlier, minimally detailed but easily remembered 10 pages later: 'The flavour of my sorbet was lime, just to the green side of white'.

Immediately before he lies to the police, or to himself, or merely the reader, Joe has been thinking about a truth free of self-interest, doubting whether a willed objectivity can save us from our engrained habits of mind, and has even asked explicitly, in a sentence standing alone as a paragraph: 'But exactly what interests of mine were served by my own account of the restaurant lunch?'

McEwan is anything but a crude writer, even when he chooses extreme subject matter, and such a sharp-elbowed nudge to the reader is out of character. To introduce at this late stage an unreliable narrator is perverse – it recapitulates on the level of gimmick the novel's central theme, that unreliability is an ineradicable part of what we are.

Anita Brookner, 30th August 1997
From the *Spectator*
On narrative method

No outline of the plot will be given here: the narrative must be read word by sinister word. What impresses in this novel is not only the author's care but his extreme patience with a story targeted at disintegration. His protagonist, Joe, is a freelance scientific populariser, whose unstructured days give him plenty of opportunity for observation, so that he is usually aware of the figure on the opposite pavement, is available to note telephone calls, even when he has switched off his answering machine. This is clearly an affair between men; it is erotomania disguised as concern, religion without morality, loving kindness designed as endless pursuit, and in the final analysis a will to extinction. It is almost a miracle that the novel holds up under the strain.

ATONEMENT

David Sexton, 10th September 2001
From the *Evening Standard*
On the theme of storytelling

Atonement is McEwan's best novel, so far, his masterpiece. Its long opening scene returns once more to the confusions of youthful sexuality, as perceived and misperceived, with devastating consequences, by an adolescent girl. But McEwan no longer leaves his story there, as he did in his early work. The rest of the book, ultimately reaching over 60 years, explores the consequences of the actions of that day and asks whether we can ever atone for what we have done, whether there is love that can endure all trials. *Atonement* is also a meditation on the impulse of storytelling itself, on the wish to give shape to experience which deceives no less than it illuminates ...

Hermione Lee, 23rd September 2001
From the *Observer*
On the theme of storytelling, literary influence and allusion

The first time we hear the hero speak, in this impressive, engrossing, deep and surprising novel, he says: 'I was away in my thoughts.' The curious phrase is echoed later by the mother of the novel's other main character, a 13-year-old girl: 'Her daughter was always off and away in her mind.' What it means to be 'away in your mind' is one of the key subjects here. Fantasy, daydream, evasions, self-dramatisation, all the powerful and dangerous work of the imagination, do battle with the facts, things as they are. Can the imagined and the real ever be 'at one'? . . .

Atonement, we at last discover, is the novel Briony Tallis has been writing between 1940 and 1999. This quite familiar fictional trick allows McEwan to ask some interesting questions about writing, in what is a highly literary book. The epigraph is a quotation from *Northanger Abbey,* where Catherine Morland is reproached by Henry Tilney for imagining Gothic horrors in a well-protected English setting. (In a nice echo, the Tallis-home-turned-hotel is called Tilney's.) All through, historical layers of English fiction are invoked – and rewritten. Jane Austen's decorums turn to black farce. Forster's novels of social misunderstanding – the attack on poor Leonard Bast, Adela Quested's false charge of rape – are ironically echoed.

When Briony starts writing *Atonement* as a novella, in 1940, she thinks it should be modern and impressionistic, like Virginia Woolf. But she gets a rejection letter from Cyril Connolly at *Horizon* telling her that fiction should have more plot. The advice comes from a friend of Connolly's, one Elizabeth Bowen. So her rewritten novella – the Part One of *Atonement* – recalls *The Last September*, with its restive teenage girl in the big house. Then Briony writes the war, and all the slow, deliberate literariness of Part One falls away.

Atonement asks what the English novel of the twenty-first century has inherited, and what it can do now. One of the things it can do, very subtly in McEwan's case, is to be androgynous. This is a novel written by a man acting the part of a woman writing a 'male' subject, and there's nothing to distinguish between them.

If fiction is a controlling play, a way of ordering the universe in which the writer is away in her – or his – thoughts, then is it a form of escapism, lacking all moral force? Is it just another form of false witness, and so always 'unforgivable'? And are some forms of fiction – modernist, middle-class, limited to personal relations – more unforgivable than others? A political critique edges in . . .

In Part One, there is a significant tussle between Cecilia and Robbie by the fountain, for a precious Meissen vase, given to an uncle in the First World War by the French villagers whom he had saved. The vase is broken, but mended so that the cracks hardly show (another literary bow, this time to *The Golden Bowl*). Just so, in Briony's accusation, 'the glazed surface of conviction was not without its blemishes and hairline cracks'.

In war-time, one of the servants breaks it irrecoverably. The 'making one' of the vase was a fix, and couldn't hold. Yet a great deal does survive at the end of the novel: family, children, memory, writing, perhaps even love and forgiveness. Or perhaps not; it depends which of the controlling novelist's endings we decide to believe in, as we hold this fragile shape of the unified fictional work in our mind's eye, and are made aware how easily it can all fall apart.

Russell Celyn Jones, 12th September 2001
From *The Times*
On style and literary reference

While Ian McEwan's closest contemporaries, Amis and Rushdie, have been rolling out the red carpet into their celebrity lives, this novelist has stayed on the case . . . *Atonement* is a novel about how fiction is constructed . . .

That James Joyce was at the same time [the period when the opening section of the novel is set] making arrangements to flee occupied France to Zurich, where he died seven months later, is worth mentioning as are the references to Richardson's *Clarissa*. It is not McEwan's style to put anything into his novels for the sake of it, and *Atonement* plays with metafictional ideas all the way along. Briony's heroine Arabella shares Clarissa's sister's name, and Richardson was Briony's age when he started making money as a writer, penning love letters for friends. It is a love letter that leads to Robbie's downfall. *Clarissa* is an epistolary novel with multiple points of view. *Atonement* has multiple points of view too, but only one omniscient voice. It might seem a pity to deface this beautiful imitation of a 19th century novel with Post-Modern signposts yet there is a reason for it. Omniscient narrators are at odds with his secular, post-Joycean view.

Glossary of literary terms

Analogy When two concepts are compared to each other. Often one is more familiar and is used to help understand and explain the other idea. For example, the comparison of a pump to the human heart.

Antagonist The character (or group of characters) that is set up in direct opposition to the protagonist.

Caricature A ridiculous exaggeration of personal traits. For example, a caricature of an actress would be someone who is melodramatic, insecure and constantly wanting to perform.

Characterisation The way in which an author creates and then 'fleshes out' a character.

Cliché An expression that has been overused to the point that it has lost its original vivacity and clarity of expression. For example, 'sharp as a tack'. Any obvious or time-honoured plots, themes or characters are also considered clichéd. For example, the cackling villain or the weeping heroine.

Denouement A French word meaning 'unknotting'. This refers to the unravelling of the plot – the solution to the mystery or the final explanation.

Epigraph A motto or quotation that begins a book or chapter.

Epilogue A concluding section added to the end of a novel or play.

Epistolary A novel written in the form of letters.

Etymology The practice of tracing the history and origin of a word.

Euphemism When one term is substituted as a polite description for a cruder act. For example, passing wind instead of farting.

Fictional portrayal A description of make-believe events.

First-person narrator When the narrative is told through the eyes of one character, using the pronoun 'I'.

Genre A category or type of literary work. For example, novel, short story, poem, etc. Genres can also be more specific – comedy, mystery, love story, etc.

Idyll A short pastoral piece describing a peaceful, romantic, often rural scene or incident.

Imagery The use of words to create pictorial images. Imagery often appeals to all the senses of taste, sight, touch and sound, and works on both literal and figurative levels.

Irony The discrepancy between the appearance of a situation and its reality. Irony can be verbal – for example, when someone says, 'I'm *fine*' but means 'I'm angry'. Or situational – for example, a blind man who sells glasses. Dramatic irony is when the audience knows more than the characters.

Juxtapose When one event is positioned alongside another, usually with the intention of creating a literary link between the two. For example, the birth of a baby and the simultaneous breaking of a vase.

Linguistics The study of language as a system.

Literary allusion A reference in one body of literature to another – be it a fictional place, a character, an event or quotation.

Metaphor/Metaphorical A figure of speech that ascribes the qualities (literally or imaginatively) of one thing to another. For example, 'Morning is a new sheet of paper for you to write on' – Eve Meriam.

Narrative excursion When the narrative digresses and moves away from the main theme.

Narrative method The way in which the author chooses to tell the story.

Narrative patterns The literary methods used contribute towards the overall shape of the narrative. For example, repetition can be used to create a 'narrative pattern'.

Narrative shape The shape in which the narrative is constructed.

Narrative shifts When the narrative switches between different places, situations and/or characters.

Narrative structure The way in which a story is structured. A story can be told chronologically, using flashbacks, beginning at the end, etc.

Narrative viewpoint The perspective from which the narrative is told.

Novella A short novel or a narrative approximately the length of a long short story.

Omniscient narrator When the narrator has the godlike power of knowing and seeing all actions, events and thoughts of the characters.

Overlapping narrative When the narrative is constructed so that certain events and/or characters' thoughts interweave and overlap throughout the narrative.

Parable A short story that contains and illuminates a moral lesson. For example, the parable of the tortoise and the hare is meant to teach that slow and steady wins the race.

Paradox A statement that is contradictory but ultimately true. For example, 'I never found a companion that was so companionable as solitude' – Henry David Thoreau.

Pathetic/Pathos Pathos is created when an audience feels genuine pity or sorrow for a character.

Proleptic ironies When something will be ironic in the future. For example, a child called Angel who grows up to be a serial killer.

Protagonist The main character. Sometimes referred to as the hero or heroine.

Pun A form of wit that involves a play on a word to create double meaning. For example, in *Romeo and Juliet* when Mercutio has been stabbed he says, 'Ask for me tomorrow and you will find me a *grave* man'. Grave in this context means both 'serious' and 'dead'.

Satire A literary technique that combines methods of humour, such as sarcasm, wit, irony and caricature, in order to create a comic effect. Usually, the purpose of satire is to illuminate the folly, vice or greed of individuals or institutions. Much satire is considered political because it seeks not only to amuse its audience but also to make them realise certain truths about society.

Stream of consciousness A style of writing that attempts to re-create the inner workings of a character's mind. Punctuation and grammar may be informal and trains of thought broken in order to successfully mimic the chaos of the psyche.

Symbolism The use of words, characters, actions and objects that are to be understood literally but also represent higher, more abstract concepts. i.e. a caged bird can signify the literal fact of a bird in a cage as well as the symbolic values of lost freedom, feeling trapped etc.

Theme The central or overriding idea behind the story.

Third Person When a narrator tells the story from outside the narrative, yet also from a character's perspective.

Tone The attitude of the writing – be it carefree, formal, suspenseful, etc.

Tragedy A piece of fiction that traces the downfall of a protagonist who is often portrayed as being 'better' than the other characters. The 'tragedy' is that the fall from grace is brought about through some accident, an error in judgement or a cruel twist of fate. Often it occurs because of a 'tragic flaw' within the protagonist.

Unreliable narrator When a reader feels they cannot entirely trust their narrator. For example, when Clarissa tells Joe that Jed's handwriting is similar to his, the reader begins to question Joe's sanity.

Biographical outline

1948 21 June: Ian Russell McEwan born. The son of Major David McEwan, a career soldier in the British army, and Rose McEwan.

1951–9 Father posted abroad, including postings in Singapore and Tripoli.

1959–66 Attended state boarding school at Woolverstone Hall in Suffolk.

1967–70 Read English and French at the University of Sussex.

1970–1 Studied for an MA in modern fiction and creative writing at the University of East Anglia. One of the first students on the creative writing course initiated by Malcolm Bradbury and Angus Wilson.

1971 Trip to Afghanistan and the North-West Frontier.

1975 Won the Somerset Maugham award for *First Love, Last Rites*.

1978 Published *In Between the Sheets* and *The Cement Garden*.

1979 *The Imitation Game* published.

1981 *The Comfort of Strangers* nominated for the Booker Prize. *Or Shall We Die?* performed. Won the *Evening Standard* Award for the best screenplay for *The Ploughman's Lunch*.

1982 Created a Fellow of the Royal Society of Literature.

1987 *The Child in Time* awarded the Whitbread Prize and the Prix Fémina. Visited the Soviet Union with a delegation from European Nuclear Disarmament.

1988 *Soursweet* screenplay, an adaptation of a novel by Timothy Mo.

1989 Given an honorary D.Litt. by the University of Sussex.

1990 *The Innocent* published.

1992 *Black Dogs* published.

1994 *The Daydreamer* published.

1997 *Enduring Love* published.

1998 *Amsterdam* published, which won the Booker Prize.

2000 Awarded a CBE.

2001 Published *Atonement*, shortlisted for the Booker Prize.

Select Bibliography

WORKS BY IAN McEWAN

First Love, Last Rites (Jonathan Cape, London, 1975). Short stories.

In Between the Sheets (Jonathan Cape, London, 1978). Short stories.

The Cement Garden (Jonathan Cape, London, 1978)

The Comfort of Strangers (Jonathan Cape, London, 1981)

The Imitation Game: Three Plays for Television (Jonathan Cape, London, 1981)

Or Shall We Die? Words for an Oratorio Set to Music by Michael Berkeley (Jonathan Cape, London, 1983)

The Ploughman's Lunch (Methuen, London, 1985). Screenplay.

Roberto Innocenti, *Rose Blanche*, text by Ian McEwan based on a story by Christophe Gallaz (Jonathan Cape, London, 1985). Picture book for children.

The Child in Time (Jonathan Cape, London, 1987)

Soursweet (Faber & Faber, London, 1988). Screenplay based on Timothy Mo's novel *Sour Sweet* (1982)

A Move Abroad: Or Shall We Die? and The Ploughman's Lunch (Pan Books, London, 1989)

The Innocent (Jonathan Cape, London, 1990)

Black Dogs (Jonathan Cape, London, 1992)

The Daydreamer (Jonathan Cape, London, 1994)

Enduring Love (Jonathan Cape, London, 1997)

Amsterdam (Jonathan Cape, London, 1998).

Atonement (Jonathan Cape, London, 2001)

UNCOLLECTED SHORT STORIES
'Intersection' in *Tri-Quarterly*, Fall 1975, pp. 63–86
'Untitled' in *Tri-Quarterly*, Winter 1976, pp. 62–3
'Deep Sleep, Light Sleeper' in *Harpers & Queen*, August 1977, pp. 82–5

INTERVIEWS
Andrew Billen, 'Eng Lit's leading expert on evil', *Evening Standard* (26 September 2001), pp. 27–8

Rosa Gonzalez, 'The Pleasure of Prose Writing versus Pornographic Violence: An Interview with Ian McEwan', *Barcelona English Language and Literature Studies*, vol. 3 (1999), pp. 55–62. Also in *The European English Messenger*, vol. 1, no. 3 (Autumn 1992), pp. 40–5. On influences, politics and the novel.

John Haffenden, *Novelists in Interview* (Methuen, London, 1985), pp. 168–90. On all the major writings up to *The Ploughman's Lunch*.

Ian Hamilton, 'Points of Departure', *New Review*, vol. 5, no. 2 (Autumn 1978), pp. 9–21. On McEwan's childhood and early writings.

Adam Hunt, 'Ian McEwan', *New Fiction*, vol. 21 (Winter, 1996), pp. 47–50

Christopher Ricks, 'Adolescence and After', *The Listener* (12 April 1979), pp. 526–7. On the short stories, *The Cement Garden*, and imagination and intention.

ON VIDEO AND AUDIO
Writers Talk: Ideas of Our Time, *Guardian Conversations* no. 69, Institute of Contemporary Arts. Ian McEwan in conversation with Martin Amis. On *The Child in Time*.

Mark Lawson, 'The Ian McEwan Interview', *Front Row*, BBC

Radio 4, December 2001 (producer Ekene Akalawu). On *Atonement*.

BIOGRAPHICAL AND CRITICAL STUDIES

J.R. Banks, 'A Gondola Named Desire', *Critical Quarterly*, vol. 24, no. 2 (Summer 1982), pp. 27–31. On *The Comfort of Strangers*.

Tamas Benyei, 'Places in Between: The Subversion of Initiation Narrative in Ian McEwan's *The Innocent*', in *British and American Studies*, vol. 4 (2), (1999), pp. 66–73

Angus B. Cochran, 'Ian McEwan (1948–)', in George Stade (ed.), *British Writers. Supplement IV* (Scribner's, New York, 1997), pp. 389–408

John Fletcher, 'Ian McEwan', *Dictionary of Literary Biography 14: British Novelists Since 1960, Part 2: H–Z* (Gale, Detroit, 1983), pp. 495–500. From McEwan's early days on the creative writing course at the University of East Anglia up to *The Comfort of Strangers*.

Damian Grant and Ian McEwan, *Contemporary Writers: Ian McEwan* (The Book Trust and the British Council, London, 1989)

Peter Lewis, 'Ian McEwan', in *Contemporary Novelists*, ed. Lesley Henderson, 5th edition (St James Press, London and Chicago, 1991), pp. 621–3. Argues for McEwan's moral vision up to *The Innocent*.

George B. von der Lippe, '*Death in Venice* in Literature and Film: Six Twentieth Century Versions', *Mosaic*, vol. 32 (1), (March 1999), pp. 35–54. Deals with McEwan's *The Comfort of Strangers*, among others.

Ian McEwan, 'An Only Childhood: Ian McEwan Remembers Growing up Without Brothers and Sisters', *Observer* (31 January 1982), p. 41. An intriguingly personal account of McEwan's interests in childhood, innocence and guilt.

David Malcolm, *Understanding Ian McEwan* (University of South Carolina Press, 2002)

Joan E. Marecki, 'Ian McEwan', *Contemporary Authors: New Revision Series* (Gale, Detroit, 1985), vol. 14, pp. 312–13. A compilation of reviewers' reactions to the stories and the early novels.

Adam Mars-Jones, *Venus Envy*, Chatto Counterblasts no. 14 (Chatto & Windus, London, 1990). Accuses McEwan of riding on the feminist bandwagon.

Allan Massie, *The Novel Today: A Critical Guide to the British Novel 1970–1989* (Longman, London, 1990), pp. 49–52. Praises *The Child in Time* as a breakthrough from a previous predilection for fantasy and the macabre.

Claire Messud, 'The Beauty of the Conjuring', *The Atlantic Monthly*, vol. 289, no. 3 (March 2002), pp. 106–9. Review of *Atonement*.

Michael Moriarty, 'A Pint of Barthes and A Ploughman's Lunch', *LTP: Journal of Literature Teaching Politics*, no. 3 (1984), pp. 79–90. On ideology, literary studies and the pleasure of the text.

Richard Pedot, '"Le Temps Perverti", *The Cement Garden* de Ian McEwan', *Études Anglaises*, vol. 51, no. 3 (July–Sept. 1998), pp. 284–96. On brother and sister relationships.

Helga Quadflieg, '"I'd Rather be Me": Die Kurzgeschichten Ian McEwans und die Suche nach der Verlorenen Identität', *Anglistik & Englischunterricht*, vol. 50 (1993), pp. 95–114. On McEwan's treatment of loss of identity.

Virginia Richter, 'Tourists Lost in Venice: Daphne du Maurier's *Don't Look Now* and Ian McEwan's *The Comfort of Strangers*, in Manfred Pfister and Barbara Schaff (eds), *Venetian Views, Venetian Blinds: English Fantasies of Venice* (Rodopi, Amsterdam, 1999), pp. 181–94

Christopher Ricks, 'Playing with Terror', *London Review of Books*, vol. 4, no. 1 (21 January – 3 February 1982), pp. 13–14. On *The Comfort of Strangers*, its debt to Ruskin's *The Stones of Venice*.

Kiernan Ryan, *Ian McEwan* (Northcote House Publishers, Plymouth, 1994). On all the major works up to *Black Dogs*.

David Sampson, 'McEwan/Barthes', *Southern Review*, vol. 17, no. 1 (March 1984, Adelaide), pp. 68–80. On *The Cement Garden* and its satire on conventional approaches to ways of reading.

Judith Seaboyer, 'Sadism Demands a Story: Ian McEwan's *The Comfort of Strangers*', in *Modern Fiction Studies*, vol. 45 (4), (Winter 1999), pp. 957–86

Jack Slay, Jr, 'Vandalizing Time: Ian McEwan's *The Child in Time*', *Critique: Studies in Contemporary Fiction*, vol. 35 (4), (Summer 1994), pp. 205–18

D. J. Taylor, 'Ian McEwan: Standing up for the Sisters', in *A Vain Conceit: British Fiction in the 1980s* (Bloomsbury, London, 1989), pp. 55–9. Criticises McEwan's championing of the feminine in *The Child in Time*.

John Updike, 'Flesh on Flesh', *The New Yorker* (13 May 2002), pp. 80–2. Review of *Atonement*.

James Wood, 'The Trick of the Truth', *The New Republic* (25th March 2002), www.tnr.com